The Spiritual Home

The
Spiritual
Home

Vinny Lee

Photography by Ray Main

PAVILION

For AWJ – who keeps my spirits high

First published in Great Britain in 2002 by
PAVILION BOOKS LIMITED
64 Brewery Road
London N7 9NY
www.pavilionbooks.co.uk

A member of the Chrysalis Group plc

Text © Vinny Lee 2002
Photography © Ray Main 2002
Design and layout © Pavilion Books Ltd.

The moral right of the author has been asserted

Designer: Molly Shields
Project editor: Kate Oldfield
Stylist: Charlotte Cave

A CIP catalogue record for this book is available from the British Library.

ISBN 1 86205 5416

Colour reproduction: Classic Scan Pte Ltd, Singapore.
Printed and bound by Imago, Singapore.

2 4 6 8 10 9 7 5 3 1

This book can be ordered direct from the publisher. Please contact the Marketing Department. But try your bookshop first.

Contents

Introduction

The spirit is an elusive concept, an abstract blend of attributes and characteristics that is unique to each one of us. *The Spiritual Home* is about connecting with this inner identity and translating it into something visual and substantial, in order to create an environment that is responsive to the spirit, and one in which you feel truly at home. To achieve this think objectively about yourself, search your psyche and find what really appeals to you, both in the wider visual sense and in the finer details, for achieving a soothing and restorative effect. Seek out the essential elements with which you feel a spiritual empathy.

In these busy, hi-tech, high-speed modern times we have fewer and fewer moments to ourselves. Snatched minutes of rest or an occasional pause are invariably punctuated by phone calls or a diary commitment. Contemporary life is also full of stereotypes and images with which we feel we ought to conform and so we suppress our true character and spirit in order to comply with what is expected of, or dictated to, us.

By suppressing your spirit you add to the stress in your life, you lose touch with your individuality and what you are really about, but by creating a home in which you can indulge and express yourself, you will find a deeper and more easily attainable inner calm. Your home will be your retreat, your spiritual refuge.

Previous spread: A few simple objects may give more pleasure than a mass or jumble. Choose artefacts for display because they have some meaning and are special to you. Look carefully at their shape, the materials they are made from and investigate the history or culture to which they belong.

Right: Jewellery and tribal masks are a part of rituals and festivities for many people around the world, it is interesting to compare and contrast the way in which they are made and used, as well as arranged into a visual feature in a home.

The Spiritual Home is about finding peace and comfort in your living space. The well-known designer Philippe Starck alluded to this simple philosophy when he said: "It is important to create your own environment, somewhere you are happy".

This book explores the ways in which you can tailor your environment to create a haven that suits your individual needs by opening the door to a worldwide selection of cultures, styles and homes. Inspiration can be found here by those who seek to create their own truly personal space. The spiritual element of this book does not require you to be a devotee of any religion or belief, it is about identifying and satisfying your own spirit. To do this you may need to look beyond the immediate confines of your everyday life and investigate other cultures – their benefits and the uplifting effects of the colours, crafts and artefacts associated with them. You will need to open your mind to related concepts and philosophies.

Inspiration can come from every corner of the global marketplace. The practices of meditation, ayurvedic healing and other soothing therapies are increasingly popular and the clean, uncluttered spaces where these therapies are practised (featuring water, simple low-level seating, tatami matting and subtle lighting) have had an impact upon home styling.

The growing travel industry has allowed more people to develop a broader and deeper knowledge of foreign cultures. Travellers bring back mementoes of their journeys, such as silver and turquoise jewellery (as seen on page 43), fine, brightly coloured African necklaces (as shown on page 177), or the tie-dyed and mirrored Indian fabrics (like those on page 66), and mix them with things they already own.

Of course, you don't need to travel far from your house: driftwood, for instance (as shown on pages 37 and 52), can be picked up easily from the shoreline; or look at the diverse and widespread availability of ethnic imports. Specialist shops abound, such as those that deal in Thai teak furniture, African mud cloths or Indian carpets. There is no need, however, to travel further than your local town to buy an example of eastern crafts, or you can sit at home and shop via the worldwide web or mail-order catalogues and have international items delivered to your door.

Opening your mind to new ideas will bring you into contact with styles and cultures that you didn't know existed and yet with which you might find a natural affinity: the contemplative quietness of a statue of Buddha; the whisper-like fronds of Tibetan prayer flags; or the soft, meditative melody of Thai wind chimes.

Most Eastern philosophies advocate a life which finds a basis in a simple and functional environment. Similarly, the dictum for followers of Minimalist design is "Less is more". This relates directly to the Zen philosophy that "man's possessions are his burdens". The almost monastic simplicity of the works of some of Britain's leading architects and designers, such as John Pawson and Claudio Silvestrin, also reflects this belief.

This book looks at seven basic themes that will appeal to different types of spirit. The first is "Primitive Spirit" which will attract those who love the outdoors and the beauty of nature. It is based on the traditions of Native American peoples, the European Celts and pagan societies. "Oceana" is for watersprites – those who find serenity watching the rolling waves of the deep blue ocean and derive pleasure in the touch of fine, warm grains of sand. The native peoples of the coastal regions of Polynesia, the Java Sea, Papua New Guinea and the Aboriginal peoples of Australia inspire this chapter. In the third chapter we explore the Indian doctrine of Vastu Shastra. This is for the hot, colourful and vibrant soul, but one that knows its limits and may need to be calmed from time to time. "Ways of Asia" takes a broad look at elements from many Oriental sources. It is about opposites that attract and benefit from their differences. "Pure Tao" is a more streamlined regime, for those who find comfort in order and simplicity. This chapter also draws on certain secular beliefs from the Orient. In chapter six "Sun Power" is the key; this is a rich and powerful look inspired by the ancient Mayan, Aztec and Inca civilisations of Mexico and South and Central America and the influence of heat and light. Finally, there is "Comparative Style", which will suit those who don't like to be categorised but enjoy an eclectic range of interests and can derive pleasure from making their own multi-cultural blend.

The Spiritual Home is a practical and inspirational guide to creating an environment where your own spirit is free.

nurturing

willow

natural

Primitive

shelter

earth mother

rough

fresh

simple early

native

Spirit

sunlit

growth

The Spirit and Where to Find It

The word primitive refers to earlier civilisations, such as those of the European Celts and the Native Americans. This look is inspired by the Celts' love of art, poetry, literature and music combined with a lifestyle unfettered by mechanical gadgets or the commercial excesses of today's consumer society.

It is a style that respects the Native American people's animistic beliefs (the understanding that everything that moves – clouds, water, leaves, the moon, stars, animals and the wind – is alive and has a soul). These communities live in harmony with nature and give each part of it a story. For example, the sky and stars are believed to be paternal and maternal, the water lily is a star fallen from heaven and the Milku Way, snow from Wakinu the bear's cloak as he crosses the Bridge of Dead Souls on his way to the Eternal Hunting grounds.

Typically, Native American tribes, whether fixed or nomadic would decorate their dwellings with paintings and symbols describing

Left and right: Primitive furniture is simple and functional, typical is the three-legged and tripod table and bowls and dishes in various sizes.

Opposite: Natural materials such as wood and stone provide a compatible background or container for other natural objects such as chestnuts, dried leaves, berries and seed pods. Collections of found objects can be replaced from time to time to reflect the changing seasons. Wood can be carved and polished to a high finish which enhances its inherent qualities.

visions and the exploits of their owners. The Plain Cree were skilled in making ornaments of dyed porcupine quills whereas the Blackfoot used crow and owl feathers. They believed that the wearer of these decorative items would come to have an affinity with the animals to whom they had belonged.

Animals were also revered by the Celts for their strength, fertility and speed. The Celts were amongst the founders of Europe and had a considerable presence in Ireland, Wales, Scotland and Brittany in the north of France. Celtic artwork and technical skills, seen in their metal and leather work, are still admired. These peoples marked the seasons with ceremonies and bonfires. They believed that fire purified and that growth sprang anew from its ashes. Water was also a powerful symbol for the Celts. It was the creator as well as the destroyer of life. Whorls, a water-like swirling motif, are common in Celtic decoration.

Nature was venerated by these various peoples and sects because it affected their daily lives, even more than it does ours today. Nature provided the materials for their homes and food for their tables as well as their heat, light and water. We, in the modern world often lose touch with the direct effect of nature because so much of our surroundings are controlled with thermostats and tinted glass windows; even the air we breathe is often artificially humidified and conditioned. By turning to a style of decoration influenced by this primitive, nature-worshipping, tribal spirit you can create a simple refreshing zone that brings a wholesome respite from the machine-dominated world.

Take inspiration from the homes of the Native Americans and furnish and decorate, as far as is possible, with local products such as stone hewn from a quarry in your county or state or blankets made from wool farmed in the area. On a smaller scale, simply collect leaves, nuts or berries from a local park and place them in a bowl on a table where you can look at them.

In keeping with the other Primitive Style cultures, make the elements of fire and water an important feature in your home. This is a scheme where the focus of the main room should be an open fire. These days it is possible to install artificial fires that don't require a full chimney, as long as they can be adequately vented. Water can be included in glass vases containing branches of leaves or tall grasses, or in flat dishes from which the water can evaporate and add moisture naturally to the air in your room.

This style of decoration should enable you to free your spirit. Like the Native Americans, decorate your home with things you are proud of and

Opposite: Although they may be features of a more sophisticated environment, brick and plain plaster can be used to create a primitive look. Here the bare, rough brick surround draws the eye to the hearth where fire, one of the key elements of this style, will be housed.

Left: Seagrass, flax, hemp, sisal and other natural fibres are woven into matting and other durable materials which are appropriate to the Primitive scheme.

with pictures and images that give you inspiration and remind you of the great outdoors beyond your four walls.

Unique character

Individuality is a key factor in Primitive Style, because in nature no two things are identical. The complex structure of the veins on each leaf is unique, as are the patterns of snowflakes. No two hand-crafted pottery bowls will be identical nor will a pair of chairs constructed by a craftsman – they will each have an inimitable character formed by the craftsman's hands and the natural differences in the grain patterns of the wood.

Primitive Style is not a look that can be bought off the shelf or assembled quickly. It will take time to create. This scheme will appeal to the hunter-gatherer in us. It is about going out and searching for, even battling to get, the right elements to make a unique home environment.

Seek out tactile and natural objects such as hand-woven baskets; earthy slate floor tiles; chairs that are sturdy, comfortable and rustic rather than spindly, elaborately carved and decorated; woollen rugs that can be laid over wooden boards, perhaps left in the natural grey and cream tones of the sheep's own wool rather than dyed. You can also dress your table with recycled glasses, these have a rich green hue

Primitive Spirit colours

Pine, sage, fern, cedarwood ... ochre, pigments, mint, pea, olive ... umber, wenge, parchment, amber, ivy, nature's leafy, lichen, sycamore, ash ... teak, w muddy tines ... buff, limed oak ... mello

isp apple green, grass, forest ... earthy

nahogany, teak, mushroom ... nut-shell,

palette ... light, shade and shadows ...

te spawood, orange-brown heartwood,

and muted ... dappled, flint, taupe ...

and a watery appearance and they have a chunkier more satisfying feel than fine cut crystal which would look out of place, set beside hand-thrown pottery plates.

In the homes of the Celts and Native Americans things were made to the highest quality possible. They were made to last, to serve their purpose until they were exhausted or threadbare. Many of the materials appropriate to this style actually become better looking with age and wear. Take a wooden table, for example – instead of having a perfectly sealed laminated surface, the table with true Primitive Style is old, knotted, dented and worn. Each nook and cranny is exaggerated through age, and the surface is polished to a rich shine, an effect brought about by years of waxing and rubbing. Leather, an essential material for Native Americans and Celtic peoples, mellows and becomes more supple as it ages, the patina enrichens and takes on a special appearance that only time can produce.

We can learn and take inspiration from the tales and beliefs of these peoples and the ways in which they lived. After all, we may have developed in the realms of technology and high-speed travel, but our bodies, with their daily needs for warmth, shelter, food and water, are the same as those of our ancestors.

A home that subscribes to the style of the Primitive Spirit will be coloured with subtle tones and variations. For example wood comes in diverse shades, from the deep black of ebony to the yellow of pine, the red of cherry wood and the white, silvery quality of ash. Stones are the same: compare the solid greyness of granite to the pearly whiteness of marble, or the yellow hues of sandstone.

Opposite: A simple, well-made item, such as this bath rack, often looks better with age. It is often worth investing a little more when buying a practical object that you know you will use for years.

Left: A stool made from twigs, and the use of wood panelling, bring a primitive spirit to this clean and functional bathroom.

Colours

The Primitive palette is inspired by nature – primarily hues of brown and green, with flashes of grey from stone and clouds and the soft blues of sky and water. It is a harmonious palette that is rich but comforting and warming but not overpowering.

One aspect of rich peaty browns and deep wood tones is that they can become oppresively dark. Furthermore, if they have a matt finish they absorb light rather than reflect it. Try to limit the strong, dark colours. Let them form the base of your scheme rather than dominate it. In a light, well-aspected room a single wall of dark brown can be dramatic and will set off metallic, glass or pale items placed against it. A floor painted deep brown will provide a powerful background to any pale or brightly decorated rug laid on it, and furniture made out of dark woods, such as walnut and ebony, will provide a dramatic frame to upholstery and cushions in contrasting colours.

As well as the rich browns, there are also those with a reddish hint such as terracotta, chestnut and sienna. These warmer colours still have an earthy base but can be used to moderate and uplift a dark or cold setting. The pale brown shades of mushroom and maple will provide a more neutral background and enhance the light and airy feeling of a room.

Green is a calming colour, believed to promote healing and alleviate stress and hypertension. As it is the colour most associated with plants it is also linked to growth and vitality. Green is ideal in a simple, primitive scheme. There is a wide range of shades from the palest, watery realms of peppermint, willow and almond to the vibrant conifer, dew-covered spring grass or freshly unfurled chestnut leaves. Green is made up of varying amounts of yellow and blue, so select one that harmonises with the rest of the colours in your scheme. For example, if you have chosen a yellow bias for your decorations, with accessories in colours such as orange, copper or the vivid reds, then select a green that has more yellow than blue in its composition. Conversely, if your scheme has a more blue emphasis then go with a bluer green. It is worth being cautious with the blue-green range as some of the resulting colours can be sludgy and heavy and, if teamed with a dark brown, may produce a rather oppressive result.

Against a background of either brown or green you can put almost any other colour. Their natural overtones make them both agreeable and compatible with most shades. Think of a flower-filled pasture – pink, lilac, yellow, white, red – or a bluebell-carpeted forest. Nearly every colour under

Opposite: Earthy and natural materials are important for Primitive Style, here an undyed linen napkin, tied with jute cord is embellished with a sprig of rosemary. The scent of the herb will permeate into the fabric making it a pleasure to use. Rosemary is a herb that is incorporated in culinary, medicinal and beauty recipes, it is cooked with lamb and chicken dishes throughout the Mediterranean, is said to act as a stimulant to the nervous and circulatory system as well as relieving headaches, and, if infused in hot water, makes an excellent hair rinse for brunettes.

Bright white natural fabrics, such as cotton and linen, can be successfully aged by dipping them in cold tea. Simply make a pot using standard Indian tea-leaves, allow it to cool, strain the leaves and then dilute the tea until it is a pale shade. Immerse the fabric in the tea solution and allow it to soak for a while. Then, remove the material, rinse and dry. The result is a parchment colour.

the sun is compatible with these two dominant, natural shades. But rather than drown the brown and green with a rainbow selection of colours, try to limit the number of supporting or secondary colours to two or three so that the main scheme of the room is coherent.

The secondary colours can be added in accessories and soft furnishings, which may be augmented by darker and lighter tones of the main colours. The accessories can be changed from season to season, to reflect the transitory, subtly changing aspect of the Primitive Spirit.

Cycles and change

Nature is full of constantly moving cycles – day and night, seasons and years. By being aware of seasonal changes and what is going on around you, you are always ready to adapt and implement changes. These can involve alterations to the material aspects of your home – for example replacing heavier rugs and blankets with lighter ones or arranging a selection of stones or dried branches in the fireplace to fill the hearth when a fire is no longer needed on warm summer evenings.

Materials and textures

As you might expect, wood and natural fibres are the main components of the Primitive scheme, and texture plays an important role. Textures provide tactile experiences, as well as an awareness of the intrinsic qualities of a fabric or piece of furniture.

Wood can be used in so many ways, either as a floor or wall covering, as a frame for a screen, in furniture and simple decorative artworks. The varieties of woods available run into thousands, from the palest ash to deep wenge and mahogany. To be true to the spirit of this theme you should ensure that the wood you use is from a managed forest or a replenishible source, with a coded or attributed replanting scheme.

Colour-washing is a technique that will introduce texture and a less refined, more characterful finish to walls and even floors. By applying paint in a wash over a paler or darker background you will achieve a grainy effect, with areas of high and low pigment and dark and light mixes of tones.

Opposite: This fine woven fabric with dried leaves, by textile designer Zoë Hope, creates an opaque screen between a bedroom and bathroom.

Above: Wooden leaf-shaped salad servers, stacked stone candle sticks and recycled glassware bring Primitive Style to the table.

Primitive Spirit
materials and textures

grainy ... crisp barkchips, cork, woodshavings, coarse linen, handwoven wool, uneven hand-thrown pots, knobbly, leaf skeletons, slub, rope ... hessian, natural fibres, coir matting, leather, twigs, soft, spongy moss ... layers of leaves, sawdust, sisal ... logs, cedar shingle, bentwood ... baked clay,

These washes can be fabricated successfully from natural pigment, such as green earth, which is so in keeping with the primitive spirit.

Texture is important because it is associated with one of our primitive instincts. Tactile finishes and surfaces encourage you to explore through your fingertips, to really, physically feel the difference between a smooth silk, a rough linen and a warm woollen fabric.

Handmade artefacts are also key to this scheme. Hand-thrown earthenware has a slightly sandy rough surface. You may be able to see and feel the ridges where the clay has been drawn up on the wheel and so understand the nature of the vessel and appreciate its form.

A carved bowl will reveal the inherent pattern and variety of colour in the wood, and a waxed or oiled surface will be smooth and sensual. The pattern of the warp and weft threads in a woven blanket or piece of tweed allow you to examine the very skeleton of the cloth as well as making a pattern of colour or design on the surface.

Left: For this look the wood may simply be turned so that the natural qualities provide the decoration rather than any other surface treatment.

Opposite: Existing ornate features, such as this cast-iron Victorian fire surround, can be painted so that they almost disappear into the background.

Previous page: Primitive Style can be refined and glamorous, as in this wood-panelled kitchen where the old brick walls have been cleaned and left exposed.

Designing for the senses

The senses of taste and smell are linked through the olfactory canals. To stimulate and pleasure them you can use aromatic plants, products and candles. Plants, such as lemon-scented geranium, which emits a subtle scent when its leaves are rubbed, and herbs, such as rosemary and St John's Wort, were used for medicinal and, or, culinary purposes by many tribal and early peoples who could be included here.

Scent-releasing arrangements that include herbs and spices can be attractive, as well as stimulating to the eye. Use pots of dried lavender and small bowls of preserved orange peel, cloves, grated nutmeg and

New furniture may be painted or sanded so that it has a worn and gnarled appearance. Paint a dark colour on to the prepared surface and allow to dry, then paint a pale colour on top or visa versa. When dry take a sheet of rough sandpaper and rub gently at the top coat until it starts to come away, revealing the first coat of paint. Continue, randomly until the desired effect is achieved. New wood can be made to look old by beating it with a length of linked chain and tapping the surface with a hammer to cause slight dents.

Left: Like wood, stone also comes in a variety of colours and textures. Here pumice stones, fragments of lightweight volcanic rock, rest on a curved granite soap dish.

cinnamon bark. Try mixing these items in varying quantities to create interesting textural arrangements, with a spicy and rich melange of scents. If you place the mixtures by the fire or heat source the aromas will circulate when the warm air rises.

Candles, which in themselves are a primitive light source, may also be scented. If buying this sort of candle select one with natural rather than heavily contrived perfumes. Seek out subtle cedar, pine and musk aromas, cinnamon or clove, erring on the side of wood and spice rather than overtly floral scents.

Living elements are also an essential part of this scheme. A dish of damp stones and an attractive moss will provide an earthy feel as will large ferns and plants with interesting leaves, such as wild grasses. These plants can be highlighted by placing an electric light on the floor beneath them so that at night the fronds and leaves case shadows up the walls and over the ceiling.

Sources of inspiration

Seek out local artisans and visit local shows and fairs. The Chelsea Crafts Fair, held annually in London, attracts craftsmen and women not only from Britain but also from abroad. There are also national organisations for the promotion of contemporary crafts and applied arts. And if you can't find the chair, carpet or plate that you want in a shop, you may be able to find and commission a maker to create it just for you.

For Primitive Style decorative patterns and motifs look at Celtic art. This can be found in many art and history books as well as in illuminated manuscripts, such as the *The Book of Kells*, which was produced around AD 800 and is now kept in the library at Dublin's Trinity University. The typical designs are geometric, often interlocking and curvilinear, and they appear on many types of surface, particularly metal. A fine example of this is the Ardagh Chalice at the National Museum of Ireland in Dublin. The style is also featured on stone crosses that still stand proud in the graveyards of Ireland and Wales.

Opposite: Natural wood can be left unadulterated so that grain and knot features are obvious, or it can be carved and polished to give a more sophisticated finish. For Primitive Style wood should not be painted or stained garish colours.

Above: Rough textures such as natural basketry evoke images of woodland and nature. They also provide a stimulus for the sense of touch, which is often neglected in the modern home environment.

driftwood

lapping water

tranquil

Oceana

ripples

mother of pearl

lull

billowing seaweed

calm

waterfalls   jojoba

breeze

glint

oasis

The Spirit and Where to Find it

Oceana owes much of its spirit to the clear azure-blue waters, cloudless skies and silvery, sandy coastlines inhabited by the Polynesian and Aboriginal peoples. It is a style that will appeal to those who have a natural affinity with water, who prefer a day by the sea or a lake to a trip to the mountains or a walk in a forest.

These island peoples were great navigators and voyagers and the sea is of major importance to them. Themes of canoes and fishing are recurrent in myths and legends and on the island of Nauru it was believed that a giant clam shell contained the universe. Fish, animals and birds often play mythical roles in the legends, and in Polynesia particularly they may become physical manifestations of a god or spirit.

There is also a belief in mana and taboo. Mana is a force or power that makes things better or good, and taboo is a system of restraints and prohibitions to preserve the effectiveness of mana so that there is a balance between the powers. Water is the chief purifying agent and is

Opposite: Sliding doors open so that this bathroom becomes an outdoor room and the bather is in touch with all the elements. **Right**: A tropical orchid is perfect for this look.

Above: A single bloom floating in a bowl of water is a feature of natural beauty for any setting and may also be a focus for relaxation and meditation.

Opposite: The mellow colours and minimal furnishings in this room make it an oasis of calm.

sprinkled on newborn babies, blood-stained warriors and those who suffer from ill health in order to free them from an excess of taboo.

A person's mana is an abstract quality that needs protection. It is an individual's spirit and something that should be nurtured. To protect and care for your own mana you should create a positive environment that lifts your spirit when tired or stressed.

In an urban or contemporary dwelling these beliefs can be mirrored by clearing space and clutter and creating "islands" of function, areas designated for sleep, washing, rest and eating. They should be separate and operate individually, but also easily accessible, one to the other. You need to be disciplined and only keep items that are related specifically to the purpose of that space. For example, don't keep bits of make-up in the bedroom, hallway and the bathroom, specify just one place for storing and using them. Do the same with books. Provide enough shelves in one area, a hallway or sitting room where they can be stored and arrange them in order, either alphabetically or according to topic or author. The same can be done with CDs, DVDs and tapes.

To achieve order and define the island functions, divest yourself of all unnecessary clutter. Start by creating three piles of possessions: one for rubbish that can be thrown away, another for items that can be recycled, given to a charity shop or friends and a third for things you want to keep. Be realistic about the things you keep; items that "might be useful someday" should be realistically disposed of. As well as freeing up visual space so that your home appears more roomy you will also make day-to-day activities easier and less stressful to accomplish.

Once you have cleared your space, maintain it by following some simple rules. When you bring something new into your home discard something old, and follow the philosophy expounded by the designer, printer and poet William Morris: "Have nothing in your home that is not either useful or beautiful".

Unique character

Oceana is an airy but colourful concept, drawing inspiration from the sea-

side homes and villages of island dwellers. Due to the warm climate, the houses are usually built of wood or have wooden frames with panels of rush matting. They are sometimes raised on stilts to avoid damage from the ever-present water and to keep them out of the way of animals.

In our own homes we can use fine matting as window blinds, covers on benches and foot stools as well as floor mats. You could even use it in panels on a screen which would be like the walls of one of the Oceana

Opposite: The plain turquoise upholstery brings a flash of colour and interest to an otherwise monotone scheme. The colour is also picked up in the pattern in the rug and the decorated glass bottle in the foreground.

Left: The colour turquoise is reminiscent of the bright shade of water in lagoons and can be seen in polished blue gemstones such as the stone of the same name, lapis lazuli and aquamarine.

Shocking or fuchsia pink is an exciting Oceana colour and works well with turquoise and other blue tones because it contains an element of blue in its composition. Vivid colours should be used in moderation so that they do not overpower or become too dominant, but with care they can be used to great effect.

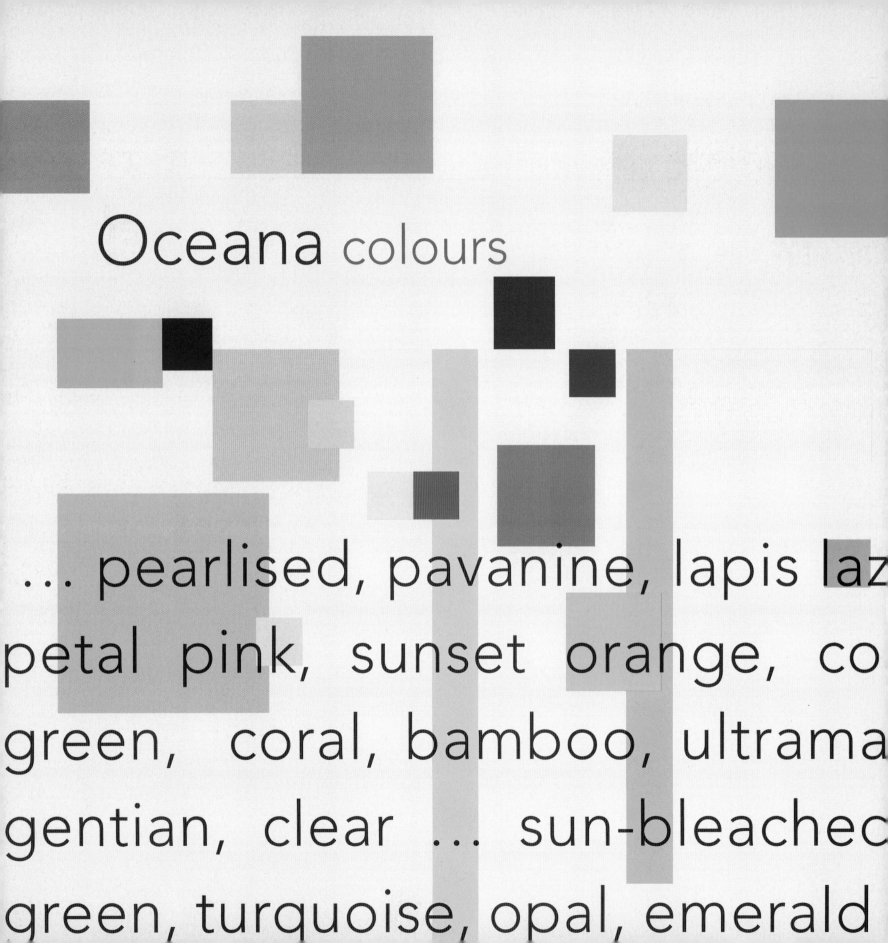

Oceana colours

... pearlised, pavanine, lapis laz
petal pink, sunset orange, co
green, coral, bamboo, ultrama
gentian, clear ... sun-bleached
green, turquoise, opal, emerald

li ... azure, aquamarine ... citrus

silver, cameo peach ... palm

ne, foam white, speckled, vivid

weather-beaten ... inky, bottle

. translucent, transparent, cobal

Right: Sandy colours are important to Oceana, but they should be definite rather than background shades. A couple of stems of grass can also allude to a tropical beach theme.

Far right: The curved shape of this adjustable wooden screen is similar to a wave pattern. Articulated screens like this are ideal for partitioning off an area of a room and are more adaptable for difficult spaces than rigid panel screens.

homes. Rush or reed matting is a lightweight and relatively cheap material that can be replaced when it frays or becomes damaged.

Undulating and sensuously curving shapes, as in arcs and waves and the crescent moon, can be translated into the shape of furniture. Look for deep bucket chairs that are round and cavernous, or the classic 1960's hanging basket chair, the Egg, by Danish designer Nana Ditzel, which is still in production and combines not only the Oceana texture of basketry but also an elevated position as the stilt houses are, and it rocks gently like the motion of the sea.

Other suitable materials for furniture are rattan, cane and bamboo. Lloyd Loom chairs also have a lightness and the contemporary ranges include loungers and chairs with footstools, which are ideal for reclining and relaxing on.

Carved figures, wall panels and wooden screens are widely found, sometimes in-laid with shell. Stylised birds, animals and gods' features are often carved into totem-like poles or busts. These are made in dark wood or sometimes stone, like the mysterious heads on Easter Island.

Colours

The shades of Oceana are mixed. From the natural palette there are the rich creams of clam and otter shells, grooved razors and scallops, mid to pale browns of driftwood and the silvery grey of wet and dry sand. These are neutral colours but here they should have depth and be a definite element in the scheme rather than a background shade. As a foil to these natural tones there is a palette of vivid colours inspired by the bright oranges and hot pinks of sunsets, the brilliant petals of blooming bougainvillaea, orchids, oleander and hibiscus. There are subtler shades too, such as the peach tones of coral and the underside of tropical shells, the dusky pink of the chest of the frigate bird and above all the various shades of blue, from turquoise to midnight, that are found in the sea and sky, and the iridescent pavanine hidden inside ormer and mussel shells. No single shade of blue is enough, several tones are required.

As this style is inspired by nature's elements, the application of colour should be influenced by the variety and range of natural colour effects. Experiment with dappled and mixed shades. Look at how light plays on the waves of sand left by the sea; study a shell for myriad variations of the same colour, and observe how the sky and sea can change from gem-like azure to angry violet and to steel grey-blue in the space of a few hours.

Fresh bedlinen can be made even more inviting by spraying it with eau de cologne or linen spray. Do this just before going to bed so that the heat of your body will make the vapour circulate. A light sprinkling of a calming scent, such as lavender, will help you to relax and sleep well.

Natural woods should be waxed or sealed for protection. Splashes of water, hot coffee mugs or steam will mark and stain causing damage to the appearance of the surface. For Oceana avoid hard, glossy varnishes – instead look for matt finishes that soak into the wood and won't leave a residue.

Taking a lead from the all-important and ever-present water, try painting colour on walls and floors in a wash rather than as a solid coat. Dilute paint or stain and apply it in large sweeping movements with a textured sponge, crisp cloth rag or a coarse bristle brush, then let it dry without evening out the slight variations in the depth of colour. With pale colour washes, especially on floor surfaces, a top coat of a matt sealant or varnish will help to make it more long-lasting and easy to clean.

For soft furnishings, you can use layers of voiles to create window or door treatments or even decorative panels around a bedhead. Richly coloured voiles tint the light that flows through them and you can create interesting effects by putting two or three colours together. For example, place a layer of red so that it overlaps with a layer of yellow, where the colours lie on top of each other they create orange, yet in places where they are separate they retain their own individual colour.

Cycles and change

Instead of the more obvious vegetal cycle of bud, leaf and fall, as found in "Primitive Spirit", here the cycle is influenced by the moon. The lunar cycle causes the twice daily rise and fall of the oceans which also has an effect on the island dweller's daily rhythm of life.

The weather also has an effect on Oceana homes, it creates storms and periods of calm, giving contrast and change. Both are necessary for development and diversity so should be appreciated and enjoyed for their different strengths and moods.

Although this is a sunny, light summery style of decoration it can also be used to bring light and warmth into the home at cooler times of the year. In the colour section we have discussed and included both hot and cold tones from vivid pink and orange to cool blue and turquoise. These colours can be used to change the emphasis in a room from season to season. Use the cool blues and turquoises in throws, cushions and other accessories to make a room feel cooler and fresher during the heat of the summer, and bring in the warmer reds and oranges to brighten up the darkness of the winter months.

Accessories can be constant in the room, as it may take only a simple rearrangement to change the overall effect. For example if you have a mix of greeny-blue and violet-blue cushions alongside the pinks and oranges, then put the blues to the front and use the warmer colours behind so that they peak out rather than being on full display. The arrangement can be reversed when a mood change is needed.

Oceana materials
and textures

grains of sand ... glazed, coral ... curvaceous shells, knobbly driftwood, baked, granular, soft sponges ... crisp loofahs ... sun-dried, curls of wafting seaweeds, crashing waves, watery, silky smooth ... pebbles, voiles, basketwork, billowing, muslin, diluted, ... seagrass ... light, airy, space, flotsam

Materials and textures

To emulate water you can use glass or mirror, shiny surfaces such as chrome and silver, or polished and glazed finishes that reflect the light; crystals also have a water-like affinity. All should be kept clean and sparkling to create aqueous illusions.

Beach-combing finds such as sand-washed and unusually patterned stones and delicate shells, even birds' feathers, can be brought indoors. The flotsam and jetsam of the beach may contain interesting bits of rope, cork fishing net floats that have been washed ashore, smoothed glass and old bottles, all of which can be arranged and attractively displayed or used in a decorative way. Drill holes in small stones and shells and thread them on to a piece of rope or cord which can then be arranged in front of a

Opposite: Tongue-and-groove panelling used horizontally looks like the planking on a clinker-built boat, it also has overtones of seaside huts and shacks.

Left: The cleansing properties of water are not just physical, they can also be spiritual, as in psychologically washing away worries and woes. The buoyancy of warm water in a bath can also help to relieve the pressure and stress on bones and muscle and promote relaxation.

Next page: A mix of mature plants with broad palm leaves and delicate finger-like fronds will introduce an exotic and lush note to otherwise low-key schemes.

Furniture can also reflect the laid-back style of this chapter. Great thinkers and statesmen such as Mahatma Gandhi, Thomas Jefferson and Winston Churchill worked in the reclining position which enables the body to be relaxed while the mind can be wholly directed to thought and contemplation.

bathroom window as a screen or on the outside of a clear plastic shower curtain. You could also construct a simple frame for a mirror or picture from chunks of driftwood and the surface of the wood could be further embellished by glueing on small shells and stones, and a piece of gnarled, sea-battered rope could be used to hang it up.

Fabrics such as fine silk and mercerised cotton, with a slightly glazed shiny surface, are suitable for this look as are finest woven cotton or linen. The fine fabrics have an almost fluid appearance and will flutter and move in the wind when hung by an open window. Fabrics can also be pleated to create shell- and ripple-like effects.

Colourful, patterned fabrics such as those featuring batik wax relief printing will add an unmistakable tropical note. The name batik comes from the Javanese word for "painted".

More obviously tactile and textured materials such as rope, jute and banana-leaf fabric, whose raw materials could be sourced from the tropical- or jungle-like land behind the beach or coastline of these islands, will also endorse this style. As well as the dried and woven products of these plants, you could introduce a living plant, such as the exotic *coco de mer* from the Seychelles palm tree. The fruit is a large, dark brown, two-lobed edible nut, which can also be propagated and grown indoors or in a conservatory.

Sensuous tropical orchids can be grown successfully even in temperate climates, although they must be kept indoors and away from drafts. They should also be sprayed with a fine mist, like a tropical rain shower, rather than watered at the root.

Designing for the senses

Oceana is a sensual style because it is based on ripples and waves of water caressing the warm surface of sun-baked sand and the colours are inspired by sweetly scented flowers with paper-like petals or smooth waxy blooms. It comes from lands where the climate is warm and life is lived at a slower pace than in hi-tech cities.

The basic sensual element in an Oceanic home will centre on the bathroom where the greatest quantity of water is available to indulge in. Fill a bath and recline and relax in it as if floating in the sea and let the water buoy up against you or take a shower, allowing the exhilarating streams of water to wash away your cares and woes leaving you refreshed.

In some cultures water is associated with energy and renewal and is sometimes used as a sound barrier. The gentle soothing tones of trickling

Opposite: When displaying "treasures" make sure that you put them against a background that enhances them. Here the white ribbed texture and conical structure of the shells stand out clearly from the smooth dark wood of the bowl in which they are arranged.

The place where we sleep is important because it effects the quality and quantity of sleep we have. In a bedroom you should avoid having too much electrical equipment as it gives off energy and radiation which may be harmful. Also by raising your bed off the floor you will encourage a good flow of air around it, and make it easier to clean the floor beneath it thoroughly, so removing dust mites and fluff which may cause allergies. Don't overheat a bedroom as this may make you become dehydrated during the night. It is much better to add an extra blanket to your bed than to turn the heating up.

Left: This large window is not only full-moon shape but it also gives a clear view of the moon in the sky at night. The moon is an influential satellite to earth and the twice daily rise and fall in the surface level of the earth's oceans, seas and lower courses of rivers is caused by the moon's gravitational pull.

water or a recording of breaking waves can help to block out traffic sounds and create a more calm atmosphere in a room. Another auditory feature is wind chimes – rather than harsh metal tubes, seek out the more mellow bamboo pipes or make your own from pieces of sand-washed glass and shells collected from the shoreline.

For the sense of taste, as well as sight, fill up a bowl with exotic fruits such as pineapple, coconut, papaya and mango and when you feel hungry split or peel a piece and enjoy the aroma and succulent or milky contents.

Many of the exotic blooms such as orchids and bromeliads, are highly and brightly coloured, and attract insects to them with their vibrant display of leaves rather than scent. But on these often hot, humid and fertile islands cloves, nutmeg, mace and other such spices are grown. The aptly nick-named Spice Islands, or the Moluccas of eastern Indonesia, were so called because of their rich bounty of these aromatic ingredients. To create a scent, lightly grind a few of these spices with a pestle and mortar and tie them in a square of muslin or fine cotton. The aroma will permeate the cloth and fill a cupboard or drawer with a delicious spicy scent.

To stimulate the sense of touch you could keep a bowl of fine sand which can be scooped up by the handful and allowed to trickle through slightly opened fingers, in therapeutic and calming flow.

Sources of inspiration

Aboriginal songlines and dream paintings are made up of waves, curves and patterns of tiny painted dots, often lighter and brighter colours on a dark background. Many, especially older ones, have secret and special associations and it is believed by some that they should not be sold or bought, but the form of painting and the evolution of pattern can be emulated both on fabrics and in other forms of decoration. The paintings of the French artist Gaugin will also be inspirational, especially those showing the people of the Caribbean isle of Martinique. Some, including *Le Repos*, show quite clearly the interior of a home with wall paintings and mats. And search out tales such as Daniel Defoe's classic *Robinson Crusoe*, the spice-seeking adventures of *Nathaniel's Nutmeg* by Giles Milton, and, for the atmosphere of tropical island life, *The Beach* by Alex Garland.

Opposite: A collection of pebbles with natural holes, caused by erosion, have been strung up on a wire and act as a reminder of windswept walks, as well as balmy days, by the sea.

Above: Shells don't have to be bought or collected from exotic locations. Common shoreline varieties can be just as attractive. Coral should only be obtained from reliable sources. Many of the world's coral reefs are in decline so don't promote any further devastation by breaking off chunks or buying coral from unlicensed dealers.

drapes

heat and dust

incense

Visions

star anise

opulent

gems and jewels

space

shadows

cinnamon

sandalwood

# of Vastu

colonial

Raj

The Spirit and Where to Find it

Vastu Shastra is the ancient Hindu science of construction and decoration. It literally translates as "the science of energy that permeates matter". It has been followed for over 4,000 years and is the evocation of Indian style. The main objectives are to work with nature and to create harmony in your surroundings.

According to Vastu teachings, which connected with the Hindu faith, nature is divided into five elements – air, water, fire, earth, known vayu, jala, agni and bhoomi with the final facet of space or akash. Each one of these should be represented in the home. Vastu also maintains that all space contains free energy which is blocked or obstructed when a building is erected, so the second aim of Vastu is to create a balance between the flow of energy and that which may impede it.

Followers of Vastu believe the flow of positive energy in the home promotes health, wealth and happiness. Balance and symmetry are also important. The correct balance should be found within a building and its

Opposite: Small altars are frequently found in Indian homes offering simple gifts of flowers and spices to the gods. **Right:** Wall paintings are essential to the style of northern India.

rooms, so that there are equal amounts of space and light to shade and security.

In Vastu, space management should ensure that furniture is well grouped and equally distributed with clear passageways through and around. If a room is awkwardly shaped then a balcony could be built on to continue the lines of the room beyond the wall, or cupboards or screens used to disguise the difficult area.

In old Indian homes, you may still find punkhas, the hand-pulled ventilating fans used to encourage the movement of Vayu, the element of air. In modern homes electric fans can be used, or simply by opening the windows on either side of a room or house, you may cause a breeze. Elaborately carved and decorative trellis screening is often used instead of solid walls, providing shade and boundaries through which breezes can filter. Many walls in both traditional and modern buildings are punctuated by windows, niches, doorways and screens to allow the influx of energy, light and air. Outside India, louvers and slatted blinds, made of bamboo or matting are an option for diffusing light and keeping inner spaces cool without blocking airflow.

Jala, the element of water, can be a practical addition to a room as well as an attractive feature. In modern homes with central heating the air can become dry so we introduce humidifiers. In the same way, a decorative bowl of fresh water will add moisture to the air but also provide an attractive feature on which the eyes can rest and relax. As the water evaporates or becomes a little dusty on the surface, it should be replaced so that it always appears fresh, cool and pure. Introducing watery colours such as turquoise and blue can also bring the element of water into your decorative scheme. Soft blue paint washes will bring a reference to both sky and water. Light voile curtains, sensual fabric drapes and throws that lie in ripple-like folds will also be in tune.

If your room has a fireplace then burning logs or coal will bring the element of fire, or *agni,* into play. Lamps or candles can be used and sparkling, shining metals, such as gold or brass, could be substituted.

Earth, *bhoomi,* can be represented in a room by growing plants in pots of soil. In Indian homes flowers, or herbs, such as sweet or holy basil, are popular and also scent the air with their perfume. Larger plants, such as palms and bamboos, can be arranged to create screens, areas of shade or even to obscure a view through a window, but will not impede the free flow of energy or air, which is so much a part of the Vastu doctrine.

Unique character

Vastu celebrates the unique qualities of the individual so although there are many written guidelines concerning the use of the five universal elements and the importance of energy and balance it is up to each person to create their own decorative scheme.

It is common in many homes throughout India for there to be simply one main room where entertaining, relaxation and eating takes place and it is decorated to accommodate all these uses. This is a style that is well suited for open-plan living spaces in city loft and metropolitan apartments.

In an ideal world you would start the day by waking up to the sun with your "morning" spaces facing the sunrise and with the "evening" spaces orientated towards the sunset. In city homes and older houses this may not be possible; therefore follow the guidelines that sleeping and relaxation spaces are best in the quieter parts of the home whereas active and work spaces are more appropriate towards the face of the building where there is more noise.

Fire is a significant element and in the Vastu home is generally found in the kitchen. In this traditional setting it is recommended that the kitchen should be situated in the south-east of the home because it is the direction ruled by Agnidev the god of fire. In contrast the water source should be in the north-east corner.

There are numerous Hindu gods and festivals galore to celebrate their various deeds. In Hindu homes these are celebrated with gifts and offerings of flowers and light. There is a shrine, a small table or shelf where carved wood or cast bronze figures of the deities are displayed. Offerings at these shrines may include joss sticks and incense as well as candles and small bowls of oil with a burning wick. Marigolds and roses are favoured flowers and the petals of these are scattered on floors and table tops. They can also be displayed as heads floating in a bowl of water or hung in garlands and wreaths. You may choose to have a small display of flowers and incense, without any religious imagery, just an enjoyable point to focus on as you enter and leave your home.

Opposite: The free flow of energy and air is important in the Vastu home. Blinds can be used to regulate the amount of light and privacy in a room while still allowing

a breeze to pass through. In India, carved wooden screens often perform the same function.

Above: Fire, *agni*, is a vital element in Vastu, but in modern homes a flame can be represented or emulated by polished copper, brass or even hot-coloured, bright glass balls.

rich, vibrant, hot, spicy ... deep

orange, bronze, gold ... turmeric, s

shocking pink ... jewelled, ruby, er

brighten, poppy red, carmine, scar

Visions of Vastu colours

st darkest magenta, hibiscus and
ffron, orange, vermilion, pillar-box
erald, gilded ... chilli pepper hues
et ... clash, crimson, rose pink ...

Water features are popular outdoors and may be used indoors. Table fountains can be made in stone or ceramic dishes with water agitated by an electronic pump which makes it burble and flow. Water is a healthy element to include in your home because it is absorbed into the air and helps reduce dryness. Commercial humidifiers spray a water mist, and some have an absorbent inner layers which can be hung on radiators so that moisture evaporates as heat is emitted.

Left: Symmetry, one of the basic requirements in a Vastu home, can be seen in this spacious veranda. The fabric colours and flowers allude to fire, earth is visible in the garden beyond, water is present in the bowls beneath the marigolds and the wind has unhindered access.

Colours

In India the palette of colour is enormous and there are few rules about which colours go with which; decoration is flamboyant and often, to some Western eyes, overwhelming. Bold statements of colour are made in all walks of life – indigo and shocking pink are seen mixed with mango yellow and aquamarine, and yet such extravagant blending of colours is at the very root of this look.

Colour is an essential part of Vastu style. It is not only a celebration of life, it is also symbolic. Red, known as the colour of Karma, the god of love and passion, is said to encourage romance, but because it is also the colour of the god of fire, it is thought too powerful for some people's bedrooms. Yellow when used as a wall colour will, according to Vastu, aid clear, divine thought and intelligence. Blue is the colour of the god Krishna, also associated with water, and is thought to be very auspicious. The Brahmin castes of Rajasthan often painted their houses blue to accentuate the white of their clothes.

Brilliantly vivid reds and pinks resonate – from the saris worn by the women of the northern Indian state of Rajasthan to the ornately woven red silk and gold fabrics of the holy city of Varanasi on the banks of the Ganges. American style guru Diana Vreeland is reported to have said that "Pink was the navy blue of India".

Yellow is popular in southern India. The spices saffron and turmeric were used to dye the distinctive, brightly coloured robes of Buddhist monks. Sometimes the walls of buildings are coloured using an orange dye made from crushed marigold petals mixed into plaster.

White is frequently found around Goa, a region where there are many Chinese and Portuguese influences remaining from centuries of trading. White appears everywhere, from interiors to the 50s-inspired uniforms worn by the schoolchildren

Even in the arid areas and desert places of India, colour is prevalent and mixed so that you will find combinations that sometimes shock the Western sense of co-ordination. Yet in the bright, unrelenting light of the Indian continent these unusual mixes appear harmonious and pleasing. Painter Priya Mookerjee has said that "In India, life, art and religion are one. The process of creating a work of art is also an act of worship" so that colours that have spiritual connotations are as likely to be used in an ordinary home as in a place of worship or at a wayside shrine.

Above: The Vastu home may be colourful and decorative but with the emphasis on inner balance there should also be calm and tranquil spaces where mediation and relaxation can be enjoyed.

Opposite: By adjusting the amount of light that comes in to a room you can change the mood and atmosphere. Here the shutters are positioned to restrict the light and to create a calm, shady haven away from the heat of the day.

Visions of Vastu
materials and textures

cane matting, louvered blind
... cool marble ... mirrored,
embroidered ... silk, padded
cushions and neck rolls, sari,
tassels ... fringe, beads,
decorative, bedecked, busy,
ornate, turban, coils, drapes,
fancy, ornaments, elaborate
... rattan, carved wood ...
block prints, carpets, cotton,
filigree ... stamped patterns

Right: Polished metal bowls can be used to mirror and amplify the effect of any candle or oil lamp placed within or beside it. Perfumed oils may also be used to add their scent to the air.

Opposite: The Indian continent has a rich and varied tradition of decorative materials. Here a fiery coloured tent-like drape has been printed with a free-flowing pattern of airy feathers, earthy leaf-like motifs and a stylized paisley design.

Cycles and change

Climate dictates the cycles of life in an Indian home. The weather can change dramatically and suddenly. The monsoon, which turns pathways into rivers, is then followed by a period of lush growth and greenness in the countryside. After the downpours the dry, hot spells return with dust and often drought, so homes are designed to be able to cope with a variety of seasons and to be flexible.

India is a vast country with diverse cultures and influences so sometimes, if you find a non-native item that has the right appearance, you can get away with incorporating it in your scheme. For example, punched metal Moroccan lanterns used with candles, or wired professionally for electric light, have a similar feel to the ornately cut window and wall panels found at such places as the Palace of the Winds in Jaipur. Paisley patterned fabrics found in Scotland and Provence can, if in the right colours, work well. Simple brass items such as bowls, will also be useful in a Vastu-inspired room.

Left: Pink may appear to be a hot, vibrant colour but it can be balanced and cooled with black or navy. The heat of the colour can also be lessened by the general space and air in a room, and will only be overpowering in a small, windowless environment.

The Western home can learn from these seasonal solutions. For instance, fine voile curtains are useful if you leave the windows open as they allow the air to circulate. The curtains will act as a filter and keep dust, especially in a city home, from pentrating the room. The curtains can also be taken down and washed regularly. Fine, fixed mesh window panels or shutters will also keep insects at bay as well as being a burglar deterrent when you leave your windows open.

Materials and textures

India is a country famed for its craftsmanship, from the intricate carving of marble and stone with inlays of semi-precious stones as seen in the Taj Mahal, to the luxurious woven silks and voile-fine cottons worn by local women in their flowing saris and shawls. Embellishment and decoration is so much a part of the lifestyle that not even the basic wooden furniture and chests, handles of horse-drawn carts or the windscreens of motor cars are excluded from some form of adornment.

Different regions of India are known for specialising in certain crafts and handiwork. In Gujarat and Rajasthan mirrorwork is used to decorate painted clay bowls. Mirrors are also inlaid into wooden boxes and appliquéd on to cloth. These decorative effects typify of the Indian love of all that is glitter and gold, it gives a feeling of opulence and fun but costs relatively little to achieve.

Gold, bronze and silver paints are readily available in good art and craft shops and can be applied to surfaces such as table tops, walls or as a decorative frame around a window or front door. In Vastu the main door of a home is likened to the mouth: only good thoughts and ideas, like good food, should enter, a gilded and decorated door-frame, therefore, is auspicious in that it inspires good thoughts and connotations of wealth and well-being.

For floorcovering, dhurries, flat rugs made of cotton, silk or wool, are widely used. These popular mats or carpets can be found all around the world; those made in India are usually a deep red and generally woven in cotton. Dhurries will soften and warm hard cool floor surfaces, such as stone and marble, which are common in India. Silk woven mats are the most expensive and luxurious of their type; the weave is usually very fine and the surface has a silvery sheen.

Silk is also woven into furnishing fabrics and clothing textiles and despite its cost, is widely used. Silk materials can be plain-dyed or ornately embroidered. Tie-dyed silk varies in pattern and colour according to the

Opposite: Flowers are often found in Indian homes. Garlands of fresh marigolds not only look inviting at a doorway but their scent also repels insects. Rose petals, whether in bowls or scattered on the surface of a table or dish of water, also emit their fragrant perfume.

Above: Fresh flowers represent life and nature and a single bloom will bring freshness and colour to a subdued setting. For a Vastu-inspired room seek out brightly coloured flowers such as marigolds or gerberas.

Opposite: In a modern Western home, a plain background is the best backdrop for a diverse mix of artefacts. Grouping and arranging is important so that there is variety.

region where it is made and the paisley motif is widespread both in woven, printed and embroidered cloths.

Designing for the senses

Padded mats and day beds, known as divans, are placed in quiet corners for reclining during the heat of the day or to relax on in the cool of the evening. In the past, sitting and lying, for meals and social gatherings were the norm. The majority of daily life took place at floor level, but with colonisation and the influence of Western tastes, furniture such as armchairs and full-height dining tables were soon adopted.

To achieve a basic Indian interior style, try low wood or rattan day beds with a thin futon-style mattress; these beds will double as seats. Another option, especially useful for patio and garden seating, is a stone or concrete base, which can be softened with removable cushions. Larger cushions can be augmented by a plethora of small ones so that the body can be supported and raised, encouraging total relaxation.

Swing chairs and beds are also a traditional feature of the Indian home. These are suspended from chains or thick ropes tied securely through metal rings that are attached to the roof. The gentle rocking movement is said to create a sense of detachment and induce relaxation.

For the eyes, and ultimately the spirit, you could use calming phrases or quotes from favourite poems or mantras as framed decoration. In devout Hindu homes Sanskrit passages from the four holy books, The Vedas, may be used in illuminated panels on the walls.

To please the sense of smell, experiment with the wide variety of joss sticks and incense cones that are available in many health food shops, Indian stores and outlets specialising in Eastern merchandise.

Sources of inspiration

Although Vastu is a Hindu science and its forms and teachings will help to create a well-designed and comfortable setting, within these perimeters you can embellish and decorate with the wide range of furnishings, fabrics and artefacts that are available from the whole continent of India. It is a large and diverse country. Homes and their decoration vary widely from the southern tip regions of Kerala and Goa to the northern regions of

Opposite: The walls in this room with their intricate gold and white patterns on a rich red background, provide the decoration. Only simple furnishings and furniture are needed to complete the setting.

Left: This hallway has been painted with squares of gold leaf applied over a rich terracotta background; then a central, swirling motif has been added to give a focal point. The rough texture of the wall has prevented bits of gold leaf from sticking but this adds to the overall effect.

Uttar Pradesh bordering with the mountain kingdom of Nepal. Islamic, Portuguese and British influences are also evident in many areas and these colonial elements have developed alongside those that are indigenous. Therefore inspiration can come from many sources and used to create a melange of Indian styles.

calligraphy

contrasts

Ways of

screens

equilibrium

orchids

balance

almond flowers

drama

Asia

matting

chrysanthemums

paper

The Spirit and Where to Find it

The ideas for this section are drawn from a broad base of Asian dwellings and images, but concentrating mainly on Buddhist-inspired settings. Buddhism is about adaptability and also continuity. In terms of interiors, the aim is to create an environment that reflects these elements, but also provides conditions that are favourable to personal meditation and spiritual development which are vital parts of the belief. Key words from the Buddhist doctrine are "liberation", "freedom" and "spontaneity".

Buddhism came about as a reform of Hinduism, and the fact that a number of Asian states border Indian lands also means that there are inevitably Indian echoes in Asian style, as well as common herbs, scents and spices.

The spirit of Asia is formed around the balance of opposites. The look emphasises simplicity but its clear spaces are comfortable rather than intimidating. This loose approach to Asian design translates easily and effectively to the contemporary home.

Opposite: The simple scheme highlights the baskets and the pattern in the cushions.
Right: The wood grain of the chest adds to its intrinsic beauty.

Opposite: Bathing is very much a part of communal daily life in Asian countries. In Western homes the bathroom is a place in which you can enjoy solitude and relaxation.

Right: Sleeping platforms and futons are common in the East, here a stylized version provides a simple bed in a Western home and the wooden base raises the mattress off the cold stone floor.

Asia covers a vast area but, for the purposes of this chapter, we shall concentrate on the influence of the east and south-east regions of China, Japan, Mongolia, Burma, Thailand, Cambodia, Laos, Vietnam, Malaysia and Singapore.

The lure and mystery of these distant places has long fascinated Westerners, not just in spiritual ways but also in material ones. Simple objects from these regions have had an increasing appeal, for instance the foldaway futon mattress or the tatami matting that is used as an easy-to-move and clean floor covering in Japanese tea houses. To the other extreme, highly decorative and lavish objects have always fascinated the West: the intricate detailing of Burmese lacquer wares, fine porcelain from

Japan and exquisite embroidery on silks and other fine cloths, as well as spices and essences from China have frequently been sought after and traded.

Unique character

The teachings of the Buddha explain that one should learn to separate the desirable aspects of experience from the whole, therefore concentrating on the best, most instructive parts of life. However, good can only be appreciated when experienced in comparison with bad, so total separation of the two is never truly accomplished. Similarly, one can never appreciate a solid form without seeing it with empty space around it. This philosophy is also behind the idea that opposites, in the right proportions, can form a balance. In terms of interior decoration this can be seen in the pairing of organic forms with functional metals and polished surfaces. Smooth surfaces such as lacquer and porcelain can be juxtaposed with rough, woven matting and wicker. Even opposing shades such as black and white, can be used to achieve this contradictory but attractive effect.

The Asian-inspired interior should have a calm and tranquil background against which contrasting textures and colours can be placed. Dressings and furnishings should be selected carefully so that each is worthy of note and admiration in its own right. For example, to show the ornate detail of an object it is best to surround it with plain surfaces. Shapes can also be given prominence. A simple round, red lacquer bowl set on a square black tray will appear more obviously circular because the background is so angular – the contrast of the two items will emphasise their differing shapes.

Versatility and change are important in the Ways of Asia style. For example in many oriental homes clothes and objects are folded and stored in boxes rather than hung on rails and stacked on bookcases. In this way items can be moved easily from room to room or one location to another and the room is kept uncluttered.

Where internal doors or walls are incorporated they are usually light and adaptable. The typical screen or sliding wall panel is usually made of light wood or bamboo with infills of opaque paper or fine cloth. These walls and screens are

Opposite: Red tulips and three flower pictures are very eye-catching in this minimally decorated room. As there is nothing else to distract the eye, it is immediately drawn to them.

Below: When you display only a few objects, the way they look and are arranged is doubly important. Here the squareness and solid shape of the two crackle-glaze storage jars is reinforced by the two small beakers with an iridescent blue glaze.

Ways of Asia colours

red … luck and fortune … cool red, blac
monochrome, diametric contrasts …
dense and diluted, hot and cold … make
striking, opposites, dark and dusky, ligh

white, orange ... green, blue, two tone

rimary and secondary, pale and dark

a statement ... theatrical, powerful, vivid

and bright ... star-less and star-filled ..

used to close off sections of a room to make a more intimate space, usually for sleeping, but then can be folded back to open up the room. This arrangement is useful in small city apartments or in larger loft dwellings where this sort of flexibility can be advantageous. These screens and wall panels are not only lightweight and easy to move but they also allow a certain amount of light to filter through. The opaque panels are traditionally made of paper but in contemporary homes they can be of Perspex or safety glass, although this will make the screen or folding wall heavier. There are also new types of glass that can be turned opaque by the flick of a switch, but this is expensive and because of the built-in mechanism it is better suited to a fixed wall or bathroom window.

Colours

Continuing with the premise that opposites attract, you can plan a decorative scheme using the colour wheel for guidance. The colour wheel is, in its simplest version, the colours of the rainbow grouped in a circle rather than laterally in an arc. Colours that lie diametrically opposite one another, such as blue and orange or red and green, will create a dramatic but attractive combinations when used together in a scheme, as will the shades of black and white

Red and green are colours frequently brought together in nature, the cooling element of the green being a good foil to the hot impact of red. The shade of green most favoured in Asia is the soft pale greyish shade of celadon, which is frequently found in traditional tableware. Celadon china was historically only used in the court of the Emperor as it was believed that any food that was poisoned or tainted would discolour its subtle hue. By contrast, the red most commonly found in these parts is not the vivid yellow-based red (like pillar-box), but a more muted shade that has a portion of black in its composition, so that it has a rich elegance rather than fiery overtones.

Black and white are the ultimate opposing shades. White reflects sunlight, black absorbs it. Together they can be used to create a simple but dramatic scheme for any room. By using black and white as a base you can add virtually any other colours. Red is a typical choice. Although it provides a dramatic contrast it is cooled and reduced by the presence of both the black and the white. But as with all things in the Ways of Asia, there should be a balance so that neither the contrast nor the background colour becomes dominant or overpowering.

Opposite: Even in a modern loft-style setting the principles of the Ways of Asia can be used. In this simple scheme the red carpet and the sculptural shapes of the armchairs, covered in grey blankets, are the dominant features. Because of the space around it the large red rug feels in proportion and is less overwhelming than it would in a small or cramped room.

Opposite: A red wall and breakfast bar create a definite barrier between the kitchen and dining area, and the roundness of the contrasting black stools plays against the angular lines of the wall and bar, softening the overall appearance.

Left: Ways of Asia is about training your eye to appreciate space, light, form and shape. It is about taking things away rather than adding.

Blue and white are frequently used in Asian ceramics, especially those of the ancient Chinese Ming and Tang Dynasties. These colours are often found together in fabrics, such as Ikat weaves, and look attractive when accessorised with a vivid orange flower, a couple of tangerine silk neck rolls or cushions or even a pair of goldfish in a glass bowl or tank – goldfish also being auspicious in Asian tradition.

To incorporate the style of The Ways of Asia into your home it is best to start with a plain setting. White is a pure and simple shade that is fresh and reflects light so creates a good ambience, but it can be cold and clinical so take care when choosing it as a background colour. There are many variations and finishes of white paint, such as a matt chalky surface,

Ways of Asia
materials and textures

kat ... bamboo, cane, straw matting, lacquerware, rough and smooth, porcelain orchids, hard and soft, light and shade, calm and busy... ... dense and transparent, round and square, major and minor, images and symbols, empty and full ... wicker, juxtaposition, woven matting ... louvered shutters, flowers

Genuine and traditional **lacquerware** is made by building up **layer** upon layer of **pigment-**stained **resin** which is rubbed down and then **overpainted** until a surface of several layers is built up. The final layer is then highly **hand polished**. Nowadays, there are also various **coloured** synthetic coatings, made with a cellulose base, that can be applied in **one** coat and left until they dry to a **high gloss**.

Left: The background here is dark but the objects set in front of it are pale so they are in contrast and therefore highlighted. The linear pattern of the wall painting, and the mix of matt and lacquer-like gloss finishes, is restful but interesting without being too complex.

which will be less hard and reflective than a gloss white, and a stone white, which has touches of greenish grey in its composition so has a softer appearance than a pure white. To avoid even these more subtle white finishes creating too stark and cold a setting, you should add splashes of colour. These may be in soft furnishings, such as throws or cushions, or you could choose to paint one wall in a single strong colour such as red or blue.

In a bedroom, plain white walls may be too austere so try a soft wash of colour, such as pale celadon green, which is very calming and tranquil. Green is also the colour associated with renewal and re-birth which makes it good to wake up to and prepare for the new day ahead.

Cycles and change

Versatility is an important element in Asian-inspired rooms. This can be achieved by using screens and folding walls to redefine space and in the containment of items and clothes within easily transportable boxes and chests. Much of this is linked to the traditional Asian home, usually a single room in which all daily activities – cooking, eating, sleeping and entertaining – take place, so the space has to cope with many requirements. This lifestyle translates easily to a Western open-plan apartment or homes where a single private room or space must be adaptable.

The Chinese calendar works on a rotation of cycles of sixty renewed every five years. The various years are represented by animals whose characteristics are said to be similar to those of people born in the designated years, for example the monkey is the symbol for years 1920, 1932, 1944, 1956, 1968, 1980, 1992 and 2004. People born under this sign are said to be clever, egotistical, able and gifted with a strong dislike of being ignored. Consider developing a decorative theme or motif using the animal appropriate to your year of birth.

Materials and texture

The mix of surface textures is as important as colour for emphasising the balance of elements in schemes that look to Asia for influence. Think of the contrasts of rough and smooth, warm and cool and dark and light, as they should have an effect on your final choice.

One of the most outstanding Asian materials is silk – a fabric that has connotations of luxury and pleasure. In its finest form it has a sensuous,

Opposite: This dramatic shelving system creates eight individual frames. Because the lines of the frame are so straight and angular, the objects within appear to have an almost exaggerated roundness.

Above: The tea ceremony is a traditional custom and a ritual which is closely and carefully followed. Taking tea allows you take time for yourself; it makes a break in your daily routine.

Opposite: The warm colours and smoothness of the glazed ceramic bowl and plate are offset by the woven texture and black colouring of the mats which act like a shadow to the tableware.

Right: The wall of sliding doors on the right is made from fine hand-made paper sandwiched between protective layers of Perspex. The doors conceal a whole wall of shelves and kitchen storage.

almost slippery feel to the touch, but it can also be woven in a rougher, more textured finish. Both aspects of this fibre can be used in one room, for example the smooth surface of a fine silk can be contrasted by the thick slubiness of a raw silk, and a length of plain silk curtain can be hung beside a framed section of finely embroidered cloth so highlighting the difference between plain and decorative styles.

Paper is lightweight and cheap and is a much under-used decorating material in the West. In Asia it is utilised in a number of different ways – in screens, blinds and even lampshades. Paper is available in a range of weights, finishes and textures, if you are adventurous you could even try making your own paper and incorporating flower petals or fibres of silk or cotton. Otherwise look at the wide selection of specialist and handmade papers in art and craft supply shops.

Even plain brown wrapping paper can lend a glamorous aspect to a room if used as a wallcovering. Papering with brown paper needs to be done carefully as it will stretch a little when made moist by adhesive paste. You must also ensure that you keep the fine stripe in the texture of the paper going in the same direction.

Handmade and specialist papers can be sandwiched between glass to protect them or applied to wall surfaces as panels with a good adhesive spray mount and then boarded with a frame of braid, binding, bamboo or light wood. Paper can also be folded and pleated or even made into origami shapes as a decorative accessory.

Floor coverings should be simple and easy to move for cleaning, so opt for matting or rugs over a polished wood or cork base. Much of daily life in Asian homes takes place at floor level, with families sitting, eating and sleeping on mats, small cushions or low stools, so the floor is always well swept and cleaned and shoes are taken off at the front door.

In a kitchen or bathroom you can mix the hardness of utilitarian steel or ceramic surfaces and equipment with the soft, natural wood units. These materials are contrasting, one being cold, hard and manufactured, the other warm and natural, but together they work well to create a practical environment.

Opposite: Calligraphy is prized in an Asian home. The graceful sweeping characters are an art form in their own right. The serene calm of a Buddha figure may also help to create a feeling of tranquillity in your room.

Designing for the senses

Meditation and tranquillity are calming for the senses, and the environment you create in your home should provide a space or spaces where these aspects can be experienced, even if only on a superficial basis.

The Asian practice of yoga (of which there are several forms) is designed to "unite humans with the universal god." Buddha studied "raja yoga" under his Hindu teachers at the outset of his search for enlightenment

Opposite: When wooden framed doors with opaque glass, fabric or paper infills are artificially lit from behind it creates the illusion of them being a window which could open out on to a place beyond. This is a useful trick which will help make a small room appear larger.

Left: The neutral setting of plain wooden floors and door frames, and white walls and ceilings is enlivened by a vivid red painting and an unusual angular chair.

and used mental exercises to penetrate deep into the psyche where it is believed the real problems and answers lie. Another form of relaxation is the Japanese tea ceremony, a ritual pouring and savouring of tea using either the green leaf or an infusion of chrysanthemum or jasmine flowers.

As the steam from a cup of hot tea will cause the aroma of the infusion to rise and pleasure your sense of smell, so incense and joss sticks can be lit, essential oils warmed in a dish and scented candles burnt to encourage the dispersion of their aromas.

The sense of smell can be gratified, as well as the eyes visually attracted, by a sweetly scented flower such as mimosa, magnolia and the Chinese sacred lily, a polyanthus narcissus with fragrant yellow and white flowers. Other blooms such as orchids and the chrysanthemum, sometimes called the Golden Flower, have little or no scent but are still attractive to look at.

Try to get hold of decorative fruits that have Asian overtones such as persimmon, an orange-red Chinese fruit, or Chinese gooseberries with their

Right: Simple, everyday noodle bowls are not only useful for eating from and holding small objects, they are also decorative and usually inexpensive if bought from a local Oriental supermarket.

Opposite: A futon in front of the fireplace provides a place to lie and relax or sit cross legged in the meditative yoga position of the "lotus". The blinds at the window obscure the view of passers-by at eye level on the street outside but do not cut out light or the view for the people within.

fine, papery, lantern-like outer leaves and bright orange fruit. Arrangements of these flowers and fruits can be used to lift the plainest surroundings.

Sources of inspiration

In many major cities in the West there are Chinatowns – areas within the city where Chinese or Asian communities have settled. The buildings and interiors of these little "towns" within cities can be a great source of ideas.

Larger metropolitan museums' oriental artefacts and antiquities departments can also be a fertile source of ideas as can films and books. In Ang Lee's film *Crouching Tiger Hidden Dragon* you see in to the interior of several homes. One in particular is grand with a central courtyard and ornate hangings and furniture. Much attention is paid to the formal arrangement of furniture. Also in the film the two lead female characters can be seen taking tea together. Other films in which you can see Asian-style interiors are *Raise the Red Lantern, The Scent of Green Papaya* and *Farewell My Concubine*. In the novel *Memoirs of a Geisha* by Arthur Golden there are detailed descriptions of the house where the main character stays during her training. *Wild Swans* by Jung Chang also gives brief descriptions of the interiors of Chinese homes as well as the furnishings and artefacts which are used to furnish them.

knowledge

air

serenity

Pure

restraint

straight lines

calm

orderliness

angles

space

self-possession

Tao

regime

composure

The Spirit and Where to Find It

There is a monastic, somewhat masculine appearance to Tao-style perhaps because of the emphasis placed on order and discipline. The focus is on a restrained lifestyle. The balance of opposites that is key to the Ways of Asia is supplanted here by naturalness and clarity. Taoism declares that man can overcome all his difficulties by following the natural path of life, in much the same way that flowing water finds its own course. The philosophy can be traced back to the fifth century and is based on the teaching of Lao-tzu. These teachings were in opposition to the earlier thoughts of the philosopher Confucius who had urged loyalty, respect for authority and the justice of the state. The free-thinking ways of Taoism encountered further conflict with the ideals of the People's Republic of China when it was founded in 1949, and Tao practices fell into disrepute. However, Taoism has never been an organised belief system and still remains the pursuit of independent scholars and philosophers. It is based on the premise

Opposite: Simplicity and nature are important features in a Tao-style home. **Right**: By using opaque shutters the maximum amount of natural light is allowed in to the room.

that man is in mystical harmony with his surroundings and that truth can be found through a love of nature. To create an environment where these ideals can be nurtured the home should be airy and free, and nature should always be present in some form.

Tao followers observe the cycles of life with festivals and mark the changing seasons with rites and celebrations. The Taoist way makes no distinction between rich and poor. Possessions and wealth are things to be given away and a life of simplicity is to be observed. Tao is seen as a constantly growing, evolving and developing presence in man that takes time and dedication to achieve.

"Trusting one's natural feelings and instincts by channelling them in the direction in which one wants to go, rather than resisting them", is also encouraged so rather than following the instructions and dictates of fashion, trust your own needs and ideas. In decorating terms this can be interpreted as choosing things that you feel comfortable with rather than those that are "of the moment". A Tao-inspired space is an environment that provides shelter from harm or stress, in which you can regroup your energies and regain your inner strength.

The things you choose to place around you should have a particular personal and spiritual meaning. They should be visually pleasing and may have memories or associations with events that bring you contentment on reflection. They can be tokens of good fortune.

In simplified surroundings the few objects or pieces of furniture that are on show become important because there is little else to distract the eye. In a room with plain walls and furniture, for example, the colours and shape of a bowl filled with wild grasses or ripe fruit will stand out. These symbols of nature should be replaced from time to time to reflect the changing seasons and the cycle of life and growth that are so important to the Taoist. It will also keep you in touch with external elements and bring fresh objects of natural beauty into your home.

Unique character

According to Tao teachings the spirits of the heavens are seen to be in the north, facing the Taoist (who stands with

Opposite: This simply furnished room is clutter free but not cold. Wooden flooring and panelling bring warmth and the bonsai tree and fossil provide a decorative link with nature.

Below: A boldly plain stone fire surround focuses the eye on the beauty of the living flame within.

Right: Cleansing, which is an important part of the ritual life in the Tao-inspired home. In this bathroom there is no unnecessary clutter, distractions or hindrances to obstruct the pleasurable act of bathing.

Opposite: Glass is a natural material made from sand, and with modern technology larger plates or sheets of glass can be made and used to replace whole walls in buildings. Glass allows a closer visual contact with the elements outside.

his or her back to the south). The spirits of yang (the blue dragon who represents spring and summer) are in the east, therefore to the right of the observer. The spirits of yin (the white tiger, representing autumn and winter) are to the west. The spirits of the water and underworld that represent images of the past should be left outside. You may not be able to achieve this orientation by reorganising the rooms in your home, but in a particular space where you relax and unwind, or "mind-fast" or "sit in forgetfulness", you could orient your chair so that it is aligned with these directions. To keep the images of the past and worries beyond the room, have a table outside the door where you leave all your trappings of daily life, such as keys, mobile phone and lists of things to do. Another ritual that can be

cool, grey, shadows ... misty shades ... p

muted ... lilac shades, grey-blues, st

sharp ... harmony, toned, family ... com

placid, tranquility, peacefulness ... repos

Pure **Tao** colours

stine white, pure white ... celadon, pale,
ly blues ... masculine, strong, direct,
atible, concordant, agreeable ... serene,
serenity, stillness, transparency...

In northern countries pure white walls can be hard and unforgiving especially in the winter and if there are no paintings, mirrors or wall hangings. However, by using texture or off-white paints you can achieve an uncluttered, serene effect without the coldness. Many manufacturers make white paints with a hint of another colour. For Tao style choose "natural" shades such as ochre, sand or slate. These shades which all contain an element of red and therefore appear warmer.

To create a soft and interesting texture on a pristine paint finish add a similar shade of paint but just a tone darker. Mix this with a little of the original colour and apply it with a rough dry brush in light strokes so that lines appear like the striations on real stone. If the lines appear too abrupt, smudge them with your finger or a soft-bristle brush.

Left: We spend about a third of our lives in bed, so the bedroom is an important room and should be peaceful, harmonious and soothing. This room is tranquil and simple, providing a calm retreat from the outside world.

Opposite: Carefully positioned openings allow natural light into this bathroom but still keep the bather in seclusion. The circular ceiling light will also give an evening bather a view of the sky and the stars above.

used to help clear a space of negative energies is to light a cone of incense or a candle. The visible scented vapour will rise in the room and can be seen disappearing through an open window or door taking with it past cares, leaving the space fresh and clean. Opening a window wide and letting fresh air circulate in a room will also have the same effect.

You need to be committed to achieve this lifestyle. You will have to train yourself to maintain and regulate your possessions and to exercise a drill-like efficiency to housework and maintenance, but a routine can in itself be soothing.

Colours

Although the structures and spaces of Pure Tao style are mostly linear and resolute, and the lifestyle ordered, it is colour that adds a softer touch to reduce the strictness of the overall appearance. Here the key colours are mainly neutral and harmonious. If you take white and a charcoal grey as the extremes of the Tao colour spectrum and then blend and mix the two to form a palette of off-white and grey tones then you have the basis for this look. The greys should have a warm rather than cool-blue basis, although watery blue-green shades are acceptable as accessories or secondary elements.

Grey is a restful colour and it is also a good foil to many other shades. It can be soft and soothing when it is the chosen dye for a woollen blanket or shawl. It is also a practical, no-nonsense colour – regarded as sensible for school clothing and utilitarian paving slabs – yet comforting and reassuring.

Indigo, like grey, is a serviceable colour with practical roots. It is the colour of uniforms and work clothes and can be put with a range of other colours. It also has masculine overtones.

A small touch of blue in a pinkish-grey creates a soft lavender. Although this has feminine overtones it is a colour that can be used in modest proportions to bring a warming aspect to an otherwise cool scheme. Lavender shades are useful in throws and cushions in north-facing rooms when the basic scheme may appear a little austere in cool pale light.

The colours of nature are an important and fundamental part of the Tao look. Avoid the vibrant greens of Primitive Style or the rich turquoise

Pure Tao
materials and textures

space, control, order ...
cool, linear ... discipline,
clear, simple, unadorned, ...
spare, muted ... pebbles,
smooth stone, polished,
glass ... straight, ordered,
shiny, steel, metallic, pristine
... dense, compact, rock,
unadorned, concrete, solid,
plain, substantial and airy,
stable, strong ... natural

and vivid blues of Oceana. Choose instead the pale, misty shades of aquamarine, celadon and eau de nil.

Another effective colour scheme uses a subtle, sandy plaster finish or a limestone-and-marble mix as a background. These surfaces may be polished so that they are refined and smooth thus providing a neutral backdrop against which the other softer Tao shades can be arranged.

In general, think of Tao colours as being a mix of hard, stony shades and calm, soothing elements. Watery, almost transparent, soft colours contrast with and dilute the strictness of clean, angular rooms – they are also extremely restful to the eye.

Cycles and change

Seasonal changes are important in the Tao calendar and are marked by various celebrations and events. In your home you can make practical adjustments that will also mark the different periods of the year.

In China, the spring festival is for cleaning. In your own home make it a time to throw out surplus things and to tidy thoroughly. Put lighter-weight linen on your bed and change heavy curtains for thinner ones so that you can enjoy the longer days.

The summer is celebrated by rituals to keep children safe from ill health. This is a time to open your windows and let fresh air clean out the staleness of the past months. Make the most of fresh fruits and vegetables to build up your resistance for the winter.

Autumn is the season of the harvest festival, a time to check your preparations and stocks for winter. Winter itself is a period of rest and recycling. Put up heavier curtains to keep the warmth inside and replace light cotton bedding with thicker covers to keep you warm and snug.

Materials and Textures

Nature is so important to the Tao way of life that it is imperative to respect this when decorating your home in Tao style. First of all, make the most of natural light and views of nature from your windows; these should be as unrestricted as possible. Large sliding French doors are an ideal way of opening up a dark room and letting the garden or area beyond become part of your home.

This simple contemplative style is the perfect setting for displaying flowers and few plants conjure up the East more that the symbolic lotus. It is serene and exotic with a heavenly scent when in flower and it has a stunning giant seed pod. The large disc-like leaves of the Lotus are also interesting and can be arranged in a low shallow bowl or dish of water and used as a centre piece for a table. Water lilies have a similar appearance and delicacy and can, in northern Europe and America, be less costly than the true Oriental bloom.

Left: Simple and functional but attractive, this table setting is linked to nature by the single-stem flowers grouped in individual vases and the graceful curving wooden chairs. These two features stand out against the plain background.

Opposite: The materials used in this bathroom come from mainly natural sources. The wood for the door and the bath base gives a warmth to the otherwise cool glazed pottery tiles, metal drainage cover and plain white walls.

Below: A healthy body is as important as an active mind. Simple T'ai-chi exercises are low impact but combine breathing and mental discipline with physical activity.

Natural plaster is an increasingly popular wall finish and can be tinted with earthy pigments to give a little warmth and tone. If painting a room, then select paints that are free from chemical pollutants such as lead and petro-chemical bases. Varnishes should also be chosen carefully so that these too are free of potentially harmful or allergy-inducing ingredients.

For flooring, wood is the most comfortable and natural covering. It is a living, breathing material that comes in myriad colours, scents, grains and textures. Choose sustainable, forested, indigenous wood where possible and seal with a "breathing" paint, varnish or seal. Another alternative is to find recycled or reclaimed wood flooring, which often has a wonderful aged appearance and a rich colour that new wood tends to lack.

Other natural floor coverings include stone, clay tiles and bricks. These are harder and colder than wood but very durable and should, if well laid, last a lifetime. To soften these surfaces you can place runners or mats on them. Sisal, made from the leaf fibre of Mexican agave species, and coir made from tough coarse coconut fibres, are not as long lasting as stone or wood but have a thick texture and a tactile finish which make them a comforting addition to a starkly decorated room.

Look for natural fabrics for furnishings and general household textiles. Cotton, linen, silk and wool are all appropriate as well as easy on the eye. If you are following the natural and environmental path rigorously then you may have to sacrifice the ultimate white material for something a little more creamy or grey, since chemical bleaching agents are generally used to obtain that whiteness and bleach is detrimental to water sources and it may cause skin irritations.

Again, following the ideal of simplicity, fabrics for curtains and other soft furnishings should be plain. If you do wish to introduce an element of pattern then it should be subtle – for instance, a textural relief rather than an overly fussy floral or all-over design.

Designing for the senses

Tao links thinking and feeling. It isn't simply a matter of placing tactile objects around your home; for this genre you need to select items and fabrics carefully so that they have a link to memory or relaxation.

The whole Tao environment is designed to produce space which in turn encourages a clear mind, yet the space must not be so bland as to be boring, otherwise the eyes and mind will become vacant or sleepy, which is not the desired effect. There should be points of focus whether

This penthouse bedroom is in touch with the elements and nature even though it is in a city. The external wooden decking with round skylights counteracts the linear metal construction of the room and the three glass panel walls allow not only ample access for light but also a feeling of actually being outside. Privacy is maintained by a screen to one side of the bed and opaque glass in the wall at the foot of the bed.

it is the view from a window, a sculptural or decorative feature or a reflection in a mirror.

For touch, the smooth roundness of pebbles or stones can be meditative and therapeutic. These can be kept in your pocket or picked up in your hand, so that your fingers roam over their surfaces. Alternatively, keep a dish of them on your coffee table or on a shelf by the telephone so that you can enjoy their smooth texture. Similarly shaped small balls of scented wood such as cedar, pear, pine or sandalwood can be found in craft and health food shops. If, after time and use, the scent begins to fade you can revive it with a few drops of the appropriate essential oil, which will soak into the porous skin of the wood.

Grains of rice can also be distracting and restorative. Rice also plays an important part in the Tao ritual of Tao-ch'ang, or "making Tao present in the centre of the microcosm". Rice, like sand, can be scooped up and then allowed to trickle through your fingers or be heaped and sculpted into shapes. It is a natural and convenient plaything and can be easily and cheaply replaced if it becomes less than pristine.

Although this is a linear and angular style, the corners of furniture and finishes should not be sharp or jagged, rounded edges are preferable. Rounded edges, like smooth pebbles can also be soothing and reassuring to touch.

Sources of inspiration

For the contemporary element of Tao style look at the simplicity of the work produced by leading modern designers and architects such as Claudio Silvestrin and John Pawson. Their minimal approach to furnishing space is sympathetic to Tao style. The monastic element can be researched by looking at books and pictures of old monasteries, nunneries and other religious institutions, places where personal belongings and clutter are not encouraged.

For natural and environmentally safe supplies for your home look in your local telephone directory or search the web for suitable building research establishments and ecological design associations.

Opposite: Wooden units and a slate floor bring a natural touch to this contemporary kitchen, and the glass shelves and the reflective metal surfaces help alleviate the heaviness of the dark wood and charcoal grey slate.

Above: Items that are left on display should be simple, clean and ordered so that they contribute to the overall arrangement of the kitchen without being too obvious.

luminous

rainforest

brilliant

Sun

orb

snake shapes

globe

lava

bask

murals

toucan

Power

growth

volcanic

alpaca

The Spirit and Where to Find It

Clear blue skies and the warmth of the sun lift our spirits. Lying on the grass or a beach on a summer's day, watching the odd white cloud pass by against a blue sky is calming and enjoyable and the heat and light of the sun are comforting.

In the ancient Toltec, Aztec, Inca and Mayan civilisations of Central and South America, people worshipped the sun for its power and life-giving force. The Aztecs believed that their world was protected by Hiutzlopochtli who fought darkness each night so that the sun would rise in the morning and similarly the Incas had their warring god of the sun, Viracocha. Sacrifices were made to the sun to ensure that it would return each day to provide light and warmth for the well-being of the people and the growth of their crops. The night was regarded as a malevolent spirit that had to be forced back beyond the horizon in an endless battle with the sun.

Amongst the surviving indigenous peoples of South America are Rainforest Indians who live in simple, communal long houses known as

Opposite: This circular opening allows natural light into the room. **Right:** On winter days a fire is a reassuring representation of the sun.

Xinguano made from a flexible pindaiba wood, thatched with bunches of dried grass. Hammocks are the basic furnishing and the buildings are often unadorned.

Although their homes are simple the Indians frequently decorate themselves with bright red pigment from the urucym plant, head-dresses of vivid feathers and necklaces of animal teeth.

Although the ancient civilisations have long died out, the remains of some of their empires, especially those of the Maya and Aztecs, can be found in cities and jungles – some excavated and preserved, others overgrown by creepers and vines. From those that have been uncovered it is possible to see the style of their building and architecture. Most surviving buildings are grand temples as the people themselves lived in small wood and grass-thatched huts that have long since decayed and vanished.

The mathematically devised, stepped facades of the great Mayan temples are awesome and magnificent examples of imposing architecture. These edifices were built without the help of the wheel but were so accurately devised and planned that the shadows cast by the knife-like edges of the structures still act as natural sundials.

In the courtyards and grounds of these temples there are magnificent carved statues of god-like figures and in panels on the walls of the edifices there are many depictions of fantastical creatures such as the Aztec and Mayan god of creation, Quetzalcoatl – a feathered snake – and Tlaloc the serpent-like Toltec rain-making god, as well as portraits of famous mortal kings.

In the heyday of these civilisations the temples such as those at Chichen Itza and Uxmal were painted, often with vivid colours such as red and decorated with jade and other semi-precious stones, but now they appear grey and deserted. However, it is possible to find paintings and museum reconstructions that show how they would have looked. The precision, decoration and ambitious

Opposite: Courtyards and patios are outdoor rooms where you can enjoy the sun, either from the cool of the shade or reclining and basking in its full intensity.

Above: Vivid colours are very much a part of Sun Power. Red, orange and yellow and the main colours for this style.

Opposite: Orbs and circles represent the shape of the sun. Here concentric circles printed on to a light voile curtain billow in a warm breeze.

Right: Wooden decking will absorb heat, but not reflect it in the way a hard, shiny finish would, so it is a more comfortable surface on which to sun worship.

scale of these sites give some indication of the importance of the worship of the sun, with its supporting cast of lesser gods.

The temples of Mexico and Central America are now tourist attractions but there is still plenty of colour, heat and vitality in these regions to initiate the style-conscious traveller in the ways of Sun Power. For example on the Yucatan Peninsula there is the bustling town of Merida, also known as the White City. Here you can buy Panama hats or Jipis, hammocks and the richly embroidered floral fabrics whose motifs owe much to the Mayan arts. The coastal fishing village of Playa del Carmen, where local jewellery and crafts can be found, has a more leisurely pace and is within an easy day's drive of Chichen Itza and another spectacular Mayan site at Tulum.

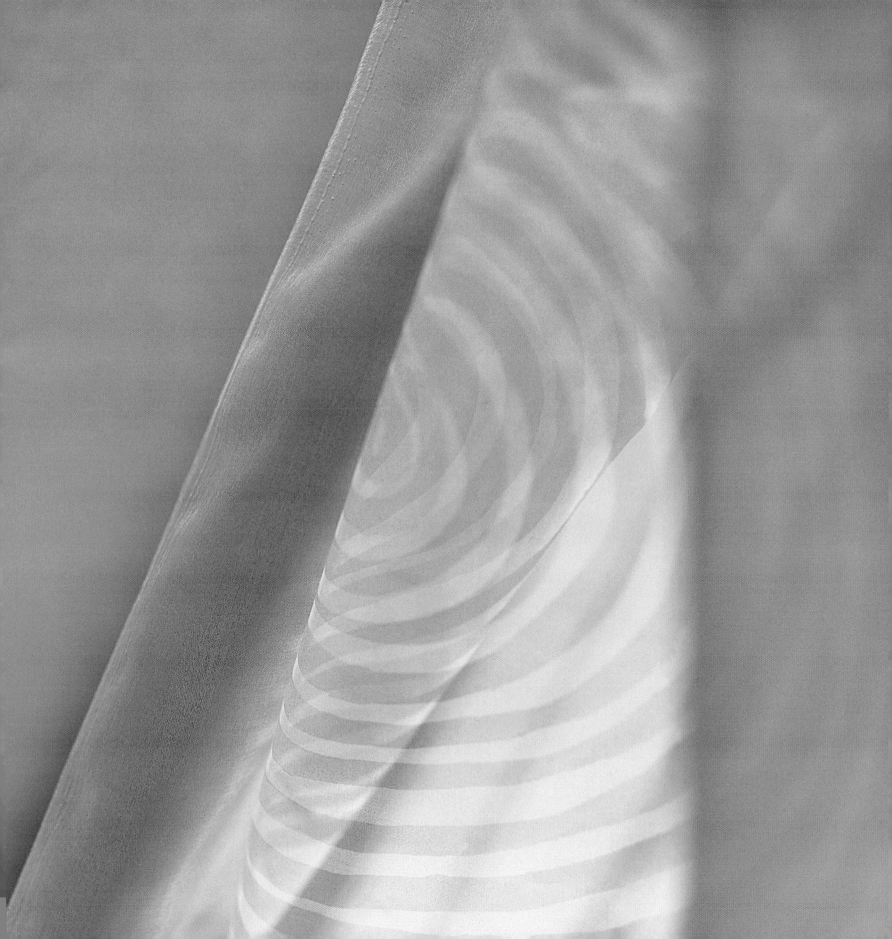

Sun **Power** colours

hot, fiery, gold, shining, smooth ... choco
parrot feathers, rainbows ... hummingbir
rossa, terracotta, oxblood red, timber br
earthy hues, rosa mexicana, Indian red ..

ate, coffee, nutmeg, chilli, pink flamingo

blue, cerise ... lame, burnt orange, terra

wn ... bronzed, biscuit, sunrise, dazzle ..

magenta, violet, raw umber, pigments ...

Throughout Mexico you will find terracotta ware, basket work and blankets made by local weavers. These blankets are almost garish, with rows of shocking pink, day-glo orange and acid green stripes.

In the sunny climess of Mexico and South America there are many fiestas and carnivals. Amongst the best known is the Day of the Dead. On this day, offerings are made to the ancestors' souls, frequently with picnics and all-night vigils held at their graves. The imagery and artefacts such as papier mâché skulls and elaborately dressed toy skeletons in wild, vibrant paper costumes provide inspiration for this unique look.

Metals have long been important in South American culture. Silver, gold, bronze and copper ornaments have been made not only as jewellery and artefacts, but also historically as offerings to the gods.

Pottery is found widely across this area but designs, patterns and tec niques differ from region to region, although the basic, simple terracotta or black glazed pottery is fairly standard.

Leatherwork is also widely available, some of it very ornate and detailed owing much to the influence of the Spanish conquistadors. The conquistadors, or conquerors, came from Spain in the sixteenth century and ruled over most of Mexico and Peru for more than two hundred years. The Spanish skill in leather work included tooling and decorating the hides. As well as cattle hide you will find alligator and snake, which is also prepared in a shagreen form, as is shark and ray skin. These skins are used for seat covers, cushions and table tops.

Glass and lacquerware, particularly from the Halisco and Uruapan areas of Mexico are highly decorative and colourful and can be used to bring pattern and colour to an otherwise plainly decorated room. Glassware looks best when displayed in front of a window or under a light so that its transparency and colour can be highlighted.

Unique character

Sun Power is a rich, vibrant and passionate style; it is not for the faint hearted or those unsure about an abundance of colour. This look is for people who are confident about making a definite statement in their home and for those who won't be overwhelmed by this sun-saturated scheme

Even these days, especially around the Mexican Gulf Coast, shops and businesses will close for up to four hours in the middle of the day. Although this is a hot and vigorous look it comes from a land where the pace of life can be slow, and relaxing is an important part of the culture, so take a leaf

Opposite: Even in more temperate climate zones it is possible to grow the plants of the desert, such as cacti and succulents, indoors. They need little watering and can produce spectacular flowers.

Above: Warmth and light are important for both our physical and mental well-being. There is a recognised syndrome, seasonal affective disorder, known as SAD, which makes people feel below par, the treatment is to sit in front of a bright, full-spectrum light for a few hours each day, to boost the system.

Light is an important part of **Sun Power**, and should be used to its full advantage. The movement of the sun during the **day**, and **seasonal** changes, mean that it is never **constant** but you can make the most of the sun by keeping **glass** in windows **clean** and the area around the frame **free** from overhanging branches and foliage. Inside make sure that curtains and blinds are pulled well back and do not obstruct the **flow** of light.

Left: In a basement room, such as the one shown here, sunny colours like terracotta and yellow can bring a feeling of warmth and light, but use lighter tones, preferably with a white, light-reflective base, and avoid too much red as it could make a room like this feel claustrophobic, and overly hot.

Sun Power

materials and textures

reflective ... dense, intense, solid, bright ... pulsing, vibrant, brilliant ... orb, gold, shine, flame, monkey puzzle tree ... alligator hide, teeth, armadillo, feathers, snake-skin, llama wool, succulent plants,spiky cacti ... smooth glass, cork, sun-baked earth, bone, cracks, crevices ... silky alpaca ... copper, brass

Opposite: While its shape represents the sun, the orb or sphere can also be a smooth and tactile shape to hold or caress.

Right: These low sofas double as daybeds on which to enjoy a siesta, as well as seating where people can meet and talk. The large vase of reeds is placed directly in front of the main light source so that the rays are partially blocked and dispersed, preventing harsh glare.

from the locals' book and make a time and a place for a siesta. You can call it a power nap if it makes you feel less guilty.

Colours

The scheme for this look is made up of predominantly red-based tones mixed with yellow, forming orange and brown. For the darker shades think of rich chocolate brown and coffee from cappuccino through to espresso. Earth shades of sienna and terracotta are also included, along with lavish helpings of shiny finishes such as gold and copper. The palette for Sun Power is filled with strong, punchy colours including primary red and yellow, used in their unadulterated form. The other primary, blue like the clear blue sky, may also be introduced, but it is best as an accessory or secondary feature because too much of it will cool and dilute the heat of the main shades.

Avoid yellow tones that have a high proportion of blue as they will be acidic. Fluorescent orange is too much of a fashion colour. Both are difficult to live with if used in large quantities. Although shocking pink and certain shades of violet blue are also fashionable colours they are seen in the cultivated flowers, costume and fabrics of indigenous peoples so are acceptable in modest quantities.

Yellow and orange are generally accepted as sun colours and even in a dark, north-facing room, yellow walls will give a feeling of light and energy. Therefore they are good colours to use where natural light levels are low. Red, especially with orange or yellow overtones, is an emotional colour and one that can rouse passionate reactions in people. It can also make a room seem overly warm and claustrophobic, so use it with care.

Another word of warning about these "hot" colours: they look great on bright sunny days or on holiday in an equatorial setting, but they can be difficult to work with in the darker North American and northern European climes. Before embarking on painting a wall or purchasing metres of fabric, try test or swatch patches in your room. Look at them during the day and at night in electric or artificial light before making your final choice.

A strong yellow may appear vivid and bright in daylight but seem sludgy and dull under artificial light. A red can look rich and opulent at night with the curtains drawn but brownish and uninteresting in natural light. This is because the spectrum of light, which is different depending upon whether it is natural or artificial, will emphasise various aspects and components of the colours.

Cycles and change

The sun is the most important influence on the rhythm of daily life. The cycle of the sun and seasons will vary depending on where you live, but when the climate is cool and the sun is rarely seen, your Sun-Power-inspired interior will serve as a reminder and a physiological morale booster. During the periods when the sun is at its zenith, this style of decoration acts as a celebration of its presence.

Opposite: These vibrantly coloured fabrics will bring a feeling of warmth and energy to any room. Red and yellow are the component colours of orange; therefore they belong to the same colour family and are compatible.

Left: A room with a "hot" colour scheme can be cooled by adding green plants and dark colours which will "dilute" some of the heat.

If you live on a top floor or have access to the roof, you may be able to make structural alterations such as introducing large skylights that will not only allow the sun's light to filter through into the room, but will also frame the ever-changing kaleidoscope of cloud and sky beyond.

If you find that a Sun Power room is too hot during a sunny season then dilute the force with elements of white, blue or pale, cooling green. Wispy light and fresh green plants can be placed in front of hot walls and

Right: Furniture and accessories made from materials indigenous to hot countries will suit this style. Rattan, wicker, cane and reed are all appropriate.

Far right: These pale pink walls have been hand decorated with simple stencilled shapes in brighter bead-like colours which lift the plain background and give it interest. This type of decoration can also be applied with a rubber stamp or a stencil.

not only break up the expanse, and hence the impact, of the colour, but will also help to create a barrier between you and it.

The other cycle that is relevant to this style is the cycle of life and death. Many human sacrifices were made to the ancient gods and death is celebrated with a fiesta, as is life, which is constantly honoured. It is not uncommon to see skulls, whether of animals such as long-horned cows or monkeys or reproductions of human skulls in ceramic or stone. These are not feared as objects of death but regarded as objects of beauty and as reminders of our mortality.

Materials and textures

The west coast of South America runs along the edge of a tectonic plate and is littered with volcanoes. A by-product of these eruptions has been deposits of volcanic rock and the creation of obsidian, an acid-resistant lustrous volcanic glass, usually black or banded. So heat, this time molten rock, rather than sun power, has provided a material that was used both decorously and practically, as in the blades and knives made by the Aztecs.

Obsidian may be difficult to acquire but dark rich green, brown and black glass is man-made using modern techniques. There is something strange and special about dark-coloured glass because it seems incongruous that this clear, light material should appear heavy and opaque.

Wood, dark rich brown, smooth and polished rather than pale pine or ash, is appropriate to this style as is dark or densely coloured ceramic ware. The dark and solid appearance of the glass, wood and ceramics acts to balance and ground the rich vibrant colours.

Feathers, like those seen in the Aztec engravings and as worn by the Rainforest Indians of the north-west Amazon and central Brazil are a local speciality, but if you don't want to use the feathers themselves then the vibrant colours, such as turquoise, red, green and yellow, that are found on the birds of these Amazonian and tropical settings, can be introduced in other ways, such as in cushions, throws or beaded curtains and striped blinds. Gold, copper and brass are all metals that shine and have a warmth in their colouring that is associated with the sun, but silver, although visually cool and more often linked with the moon, is another metal that is widely used. Fine silverwork, especially from the area of Taxco, is found in decorative objects and filigree overlay.

Whereas the shapes for Tao style were very angular and straight, here the predominant shape is round. Orbs and globes that mimic the shape of

Direct sunlight shining straight through a window is the strongest, casting shadows and causing dazzling reflections. To avoid this you can diffuse and soften the rays by passing them through a filter such as a voile curtain, frosted glass, blinds or screens.

By choosing pale colours for the furnishings and paintwork in your home you will also be able to encourage a certain amount of reflected light. Although there are many benefits to the warmth and light of the sun there are times when it may need to be regulated to avoid glare and headaches.

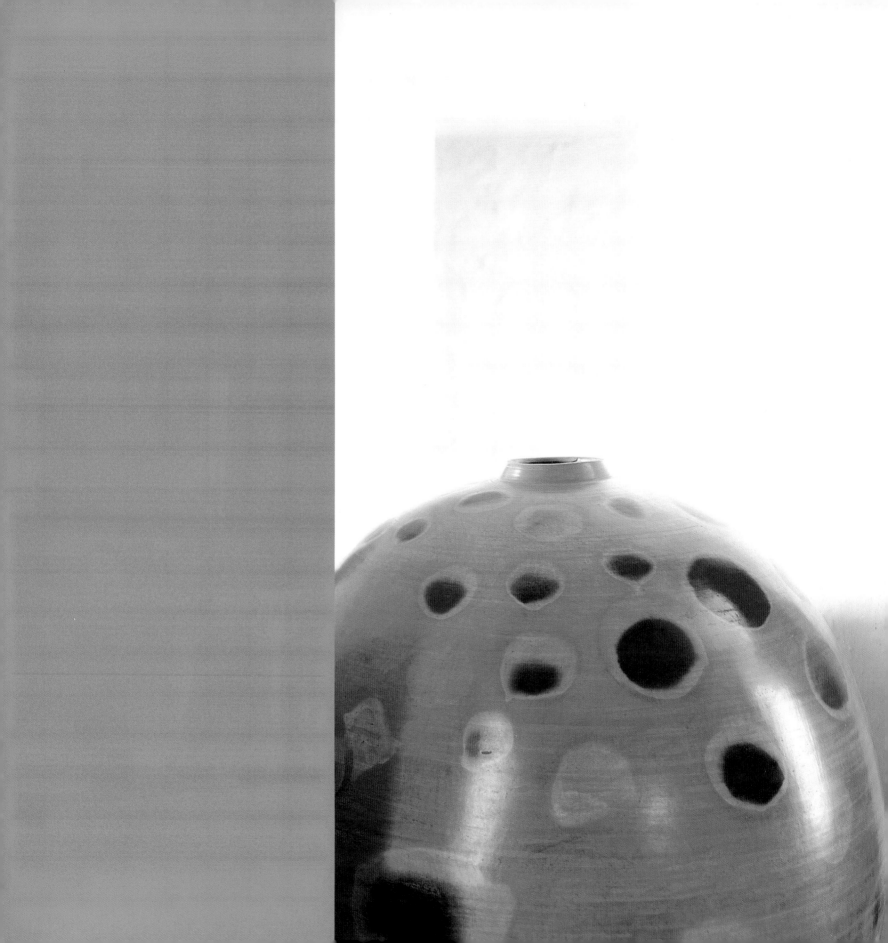

the sun and smooth, curving shapes that are soft and sensuous like a snake, are also very much a part of the overall look.

Cacti and other succulent plants are the perfect accessory for this scheme. These plants are associated with deserts and dry places and it is the blue grey maguey cactus from which the quintessentially Mexican drink tequila is produced.

South America is a country of contrasts from the snow-capped tips of the Andes to the powerful River Amazon, which contains around a fifth of the planet's water. There are deserts such as the Atacama which is the world's driest, as well as moist and verdant rainforests, so you can focus upon a single element of these various and diverse countries and use it as a basis for your scheme.

Designing for the senses

Warmth encourages aromas and scents to rise and mingle in the air so these will be very effective in a well-heated and ventilated environment. The scents associated with this genre of lifestyle are often heavy, rich and musky, like vanilla, so they should be used sparingly; otherwise they will become overpowering and sickening. Orange, lime, fig, apricot and melon scents are fresh and fruity and can provide a more zesty note to a room.

Oils may be used as a vehicle or mixed with other perfumes to create a blend which can be dripped on to an absorbent cardboard or thick-paper ring, which may be placed above a lightbulb or heat source, so that it warms and releases the aromas. Oils can also be used on their own, for example almond oil, palm nut or pequi fruit oils can be used to soften and lubricate the skin. Some have the added bonus of giving protection against mosquitoes. The wood used in furniture for this style should be smooth and shiny, not high gloss like lacquer but polished and sleek to touch.

Llamas, quanacos and alpacas, distant relations of the camel, are indigenous to South America and are among the few animals to have been domesticated by the ancient peoples of the region. The silky, fine, long wool of these animals is used to make fine shawls and throws as well as thicker, chunkier blankets and covers. It can be found in natural colours such as brown, grey and cream but is more often dyed to brighter shades and used in patterned weaving and knitting. Items made from these wools have a variety of finishes and textures. All have an intrinsic spiritual as well a physical link with the country.

Opposite: Pottery for Sun Power is not the fine porcelain of Tao or Ways of Asia. It should be chunky, robust and in strong colours. Black ware, with a slight metallic sheen, is common in South America; cooking pots as well as bowls and plates are made with this finish. Large pots for storing water and grain are also common.

Right: Cacti come in a wide range of shapes and sizes, some with needle-like spikes, others with a fine downy covering. They are an instantly recognisable feature of a hot climate. Their weird shapes make them an interesting feature.

Opposite: In this contemporary setting Sun Power colours have been used to bring warmth to a minimally furnished room.

Sources of inspiration

The work of artists Diego Rivera and Frieda Kahlo and their home Casa Azul – The Blue House – on the outskirts of Mexico City are fertile sources of inspiration. Rivera's murals such as *The Totonac Civilisation*, *The Huastec Civilisation* and *The Tarascan* from the collection in the Placio Nacional in Mexico City are inspiring as are the works of Santa Fe artist Georgia O'Keefe.

South America is featured in the epic train journey taken by Paul Theroux from Boston to Patagonia which is detailed in his book *The Old Patagonia Express*. Also, the works of Gabriel Garcia Marquez and Isabel Allende, especially her novel *The House of the Spirits*, give an insight into life and culture in Latin America.

nomad

philosophy

harmony

Comparative

motif

universal

complete

traveller

world-wide

themes

Style

fusion

mingle

The Spirit and Where to Find It

This is an eclectic style, borrowing freely from various sources, taking elements from a number of doctrines and putting them together in a setting that is unrelated to their origin. There is something of the Bohemian in this look, in that it defies prevailing conventions of interior design fashion and the emphasis on order and coordination.

Comparative Style represents a cultural and spiritual melting pot – the embodiment of the phrase "global village". For this look each item is selected for its intrinsic appeal and its "spirit" or personal meaning, not because it harmonises or blends with a colour scheme. It is the contrast and comparison between the diverse elements that creates the power and interest in here.

There are common threads running through the traditions and beliefs of the various peoples and cultures in the world. Peoples living on opposite sides of the world and speaking different languages, have

Opposite: Cameroon headdress above a mantle. **Right:** Display stands give these artefacts added significance.

rainbow, multi, many, various, num

green, mauve ... lilac, cherry, brow

triangle ... rows, lines, blocks, ble

blend, brew ... medley, union ... var

Comparative Style

colours and textures

ous ... red, white, orange ... blue

blue, black ... spotty, stripy, square

nds ... melange, amalgamation ..

ety, diverse palette, limitless ...

nevertheless worshipped the same basic deities, such as heat, light, wind, rain, sun and moon. Many also shared a respect for animals and their associated powers or characteristics.

There are many artefacts that come from different countries that evoke mystical figures or gods in much the same ways. Similar tribal masks are found in cultures as far apart as Africa, North America, Asia and Mongolia.

By collecting and displaying objects not normally seen together you will be able to study the variety and the fascinating differences that distinguish one from the other. This will throw new light on objects that may otherwise be taken for granted. There can be harmony between such apparently disparate pieces as a roughly adzed African bowl laid next to the smooth polished cedar of Lebanon box, a blue-and-white painted pottery bowl from China next to a Delft tile from Holland or a piece of Ikat fabric from Japan beside one from India.

Comparative style requires an open mind, a freedom of spirit and an enquiring disposition. This is a look that is found in the homes of travellers, missionaries, colonial settlers and expatriots who took their cultures, religions and ideas abroad and in turn absorbed foreign influences. It is also associated with the homes of artists, writers and modern nomads.

The modern nomad changes profession, home and country often, adapting to the lifestyle wherever he or she "makes camp". Their essential packing includes items that make a strange location homey, for example a rug or throw, a candle to scent the room, photographs of friends and family and artefacts from previous homes.

Sourcing materials for this style of decorating need not involve a great deal of travel. With increasing globalisation there are often local shops and stores that stock interesting and unusual items from faraway places. China and India have long exported goods to the West and now furnishings and artefacts from more remote locations are making their way into Western homes: ornate metalwork from Laos, carved hardwood bowls from Mozambique, sandstone figures from Kampuchea, naïve art from Haiti.

Opposite: This room is a riot of colour and a mix of diverse artefacts, from the framed damask on the wall, to Provençal-style prints and ikats – all brought together by a colour scheme based on pink and yellow.

Above: Yellow is a warm and rich colour but it changes in tone in artificial light, so try a patch of colour, in both natural and artificial light, before painting a whole wall.

Right: Beads and silver were used as currency in early civilizations. Settlers in North America used tubular white and mauve Wampum shells, threaded into collars or belts, and in the hill tribes of north Vietnam silver coins in decorative head-dresses and necklaces were part of a young girl's dowry.

Opposite: Tribal masks and figures are a feature of this room. Masks can be found in many regions of the world and are used to disguise, transform or define the person wearing them. They have been part of primitive ceremonies for thousands of years.

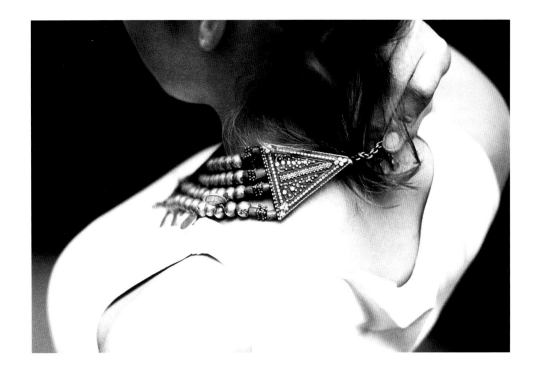

Wars, conflicts, famine and economic pressures have all forced people to emigrate from their homelands and settle elsewhere. Greek and Turkish communities are found around Sydney in Australia; the Irish have a large presence in America, especially around the east coast city of Boston, and Italian communities are found in many leading cities such as New York and London. In large cities there are often "towns" such as the Chinatowns of New York, San Francisco and London where large ethnic communities have settled. Shops in these areas sell products that have been imported for use by that community. They are good places to visit for a taste of the country of origin as well as to gather new ideas and inspiration.

The success of the Internet and mail-order has opened up the world to the shopper and given the opportunity to browse without ever leaving home. Auctions and sales are a good source of material, especially if there are items from the home of a traveller or someone who has lived abroad and collected foreign artefacts. Auction houses, such as Sotheby's and Christie's have special sales of art and furniture from different cultures.

If you do travel to exotic locations, larger items such as a piece of furniture, may be difficult to carry back or too expensive to ship or export. Fabric, however, is light and easy to fold flat, or wrap around a fragile piece of pottery or glass that you have bought. Fabrics can be used in many

ways – a wallhanging, curtains, a throw, cushion covers – so that no matter how small the piece it can serve a function in your comparative scheme. Comparative Style can also be the way to bring together a look that is from a single yet culturally diverse country, such as India, Africa or China. In India there are twenty-five states, fourteen official languages and an enormous range of customs, so it would be impossible to create one true Indian look. However, it would be possible to devise a hybrid or an overall style that would evoke its national ethos to an outsider. With Comparative Style you can incorporate elements from all regions and cultures within the country or have the option of concentrating on the diverse elements of one area alone.

Unique character

Although images of the hippy lifestyle of the 1960s may initially come to mind when thinking about Comparative Style, it is a positive and eclectic look that is linked to travel and exploration rather than "grunge" or junk. The effect is deliberate. Furniture and artefacts should be a mix of old and new, but neither tatty nor kitsch. A classic Charles Eames chair, for example, may sit next to a carved African stool and a pair of Matthew Hilton silver candlesticks can be next to a painted Javanese tribal mask.

It is an adaptable style that suits most lifestyles and locations. Each setting where this look is found is unique because it depends entirely on the taste and interests of the person who has collected and assembled it. That person will have done so for his or her own pleasure and interest, not to follow any particular fashion. Rather than being a spiritual style it is a style of spirits.

Above: An ornately carved bed head and side cabinet from Hong Kong are at home in a contemporary-style London house.

Opposite: A classic Georgian hall-way in a house in Dublin provides a serene setting for a collection of painted wooden temple monks brought back by the homeowner from a trip to the Far East.

Smaller items need to be carefully grouped and displayed, otherwise they can be lost in a sea of larger pieces. Firstly, they can be arranged according to size. Place taller items to the back and smaller pieces in front so that all can be clearly seen. Elevate items on stands, either made out of blocks of wood, Perspex or stone, to make them more noticeable. Place items on a shelf or mantelpiece to give them prominence. Wall-mounted display cases or sub-divided boxes are also worth considering. These can be filled with a selection of items such as brass opium weights from Thailand, or jade, ivory and wood Japanese netsuke toggles, once used to fasten a purse or fan to a kimono, can be interestingly arranged.

Lighting also plays an important role. Target or spot lighting can be used to highlight certain special items, leaving others in the background or a less prominent position, until the objects or lighting is rearranged and the focus is directed on to something else.

Colours

All colour and any colour is appropriate to this melting-pot of styles and its mix of artefacts, finishes and fabrics, but various elements can be brought together to form small tableaux or a more regular arrangement if themed by colour. This will also help to give a less jumbled, more cohesive look.

The easiest way to start with a scheme like this is to choose a plain background for your room and to let the accessories and decorative items bring in the colour, form and pattern. The walls can be dramatic in black or dark brown, or simple and fresh in white; a lot will depend on the basis of your style. Where possible opt for a plain floor so that it can be dressed with rugs.

Colour theming also helps bring together diverse elements. For example, black and red are often paired because the dark tone calms the vivid hue. This combination appears in the artwork and accessories of many different cultures, for example the lacquerware found in China and Burma, kilims and carpets from Uzbekistan and northern India. Red is often found in the dyed feathers of tribal headdresses from South America and black is a common colour for leather upholstery in furniture from the 1950s and '60s, such as the classic Corbusier recliner. Put

Opposite: A bed surround has been constructed in a Western home to accommodate traditional Eastern hangings and the colour scheme for the room has been chosen to complement the colours of the fabric's embroidery.

Below: A patchwork fringe of flag- or pennant-like shapes uses a rainbow range of colours and a diverse selection of patterns.

Below: Fabrics are the easiest mementoes to bring home from abroad. They can be used as floor coverings, throws, cushion covers or wall hangings.

Opposite: Here a panel of old, hand-crafted material, probably worn originally as a wrap or other simple garment, is hung from a spear which ties in with the primitive roots of the cloth.

together in one room, all these items would be compatible.

Another scheme could revolve around blue, white and green which is a light, fresh palette. Blue and white china can be found in Morocco as well as in English willow pattern plate; the soft green of celadon is found in jade and certain types of soapstone. Blue and white features in many dyed and printed fabrics, from Provence in the South of France to the block-printed cottons of Rajasthan in India.

Materials and textures

Sari silks are beautiful and some can be very fine and voile-like. They often have deep, decorative borders, sometimes embroidered with gold, these make wonderful dressings for bedheads, windows and doorways.

Ikat is the name given to a style of fabric printing that is found widely across Central Asia and some parts of Africa. The ikat technique is known as *asab* in Arabic, *ipekshahi* in Turkish and *patola* in Hindi. With its far-reaching appeal and broad base of production it is an ideal fabric for a room of Comparative Style.

The single feature shared by all ikat fabrics is the complex dying process. Either the warp thread (which runs from top to bottom) or the weft (which runs from side to side) is selectively dyed before weaving so that part of it is stained with colour. In simple ikats this colour is usually indigo and the other part remains white or plain. In more complex patterns, three or four dyings may take place, each in a different colour so that the single thread is rainbow-like. This is known as reserve or resist dying. Once the weaving starts, the undyed and dyed threads meet to produce a soft, almost blurry pattern, which explains why the word *abr* – meaning cloud – was used to describe it by the Persians. Patterns of Ikat are usually angular, including diamond and zig-zag shapes.

Like Ikat fabrics, flat-weave cotton rugs and mats such as dhurries and kilims come from a broad variety of geographical sources. Many dhurries come from India but there are rugs in this style woven in Poland and Romania, often with more contemporary or floral motifs. Kilims are oriental tapestry rugs originally from Persia, then Turkey, now also produced in China and other countries.

Other floorcoverings, such as those made from indigenous natural fibres such as jute, coir and sisal, are also universal. These range from the tatami matting of Japanese tea-houses, to chatais of India and the palm-and-banana-leaf mats of Polynesia.

Above: A basket overflowing with wooden and shell necklaces adds a feeling of opulence to a room.

Opposite: A contemporary ethnic painting has provided the rich and colourful base for the scheme of this room which includes a mirrored cushion cover edged with cowrie shells, an Indian style embroidered cover and modern Western upholstery fabric.

Designing for the senses

As this style is multi-cultural you can please yourself and pamper your own whims with a selection of sensual elements from around the globe. Choose indulgent textures such as silk and cashmere, perfumes from woody sandalwood and patchouli to jasmine and cinnamon. Diffuse candlelight through pierced metal Moroccan shades or punched terracotta holders from Italy. The world is your oyster. You can select the best from each continent while still being true to your vision.

For your taste buds experiment with fusion cooking. This started in Australia where Malay and Thai influences permeated traditional local recipes and the two styles and countries' various ingredients became mixed.

Sources of inspiration

Look at the collections and homes of great travellers. Collections are often left to museums or the homes they belonged in have been opened as museums in their own right. The amazing building where Isabella Stewart Gardner lived at Fenway in Boston is a wonderful example of Comparative Style. Externally, the building is in the Venetian palazzo style. Inside there are over two thousand eclectic artefacts ranged over four floors. Everything remains as it was on her death in 1924.

Another destination worth a look, although less grand in scale, is the Château de Monte-Cristo near St-Germain-en-Laye, on the outskirts of Paris. This house was home to the writer Alexandre Dumas and has a magnificent Moorish salon, complete with arches and stained glass.

You can also draw inspiration from the previous chapters in this book. Pick and choose elements that appeal to you from each. Look for colours that you feel are restful, objects that are of interest and concepts that intrigue and entertain you. Blend them together to form your own unique style. Your spiritual home is, after all, where your spirit feels at rest and this book has explored how to open doors to a world of inspiration, with ideas from cultures, styles and homes all over the world.

Index

Page numbers in *italics* refer to captions.

Credits

All pictures are by Ray Main. The following images are reproduced with the kind permission of:

p21/26 designer Roger Oates; p28/130 architects McDowel & Benedetti; p 49 Usick Heal Associates; p51 Great Eastern Hotel; p90 designer Alidad; p92 designer Isokon; p96 architect John Pawson; p102 designer Kate Blee; p104/105 Peter Wadley architects; p106 John Minshaw Designs; p112 architect Chris Cowper; p113 designer Nick Allen; p114/145/134 Plain and Simple Kitchens; p115 designer Kelly Hoppen; p129 architect Mark Guard; p137 architect Spencer Fung; p142/143 architect Simon Condor; p146 C2 architects; p148 architect Mark Lee; p150 designer Nana Ditzel; p153 designer Jan Milne; p158 architect Charles Rutherford; p178/179 designer Natalie Hambro; p183 architect Brian Ma-Siy.

The publishers would like to thank the following people without whom this book could not have been made:

for **props** David Wainwright, 63 Portobello Road, London W11 3DB, T.020 7727 0707/F.020 7221 9181 and 251 Portobello Road, London W11 1LT, T.020 7792 1988; Gong, 182 Portobello Rd, London, W11 2EB,T.020 7565 4162, F.020 7565 4225, email joplismy@hotmail.com; Graham & Green, 4,7,10, Elgin Crescent, London W11 2JA, T.020 7727 4594, F.020 7229 9717, www.grahamandgreen.co.uk; for the **hand-made basin** on page 55 Darshana Raja, T.020 7794 1121/T.020 7916 9794, e-mail darshanaraja@aol.com; Ray Main and his assistant Sophie Munroe for exquisite **photography**; Owen Gale at **Mainstream** for his unending patient support; Charlotte Cave for faultless **styling**; Ana Krnajski and Peter Adler; **models** Lotte Oldfield and Sue Bithel; **designer** Molly Shields for her magic touch; Anderley Moore for copyediting and Helen Snaithe for the index.